REAL ESTATE INVESTING MASTERY

2-IN-1 BEGINNER'S BOOK

ACHIEVE FINANCIAL FREEDOM WITH RENTAL
PROPERTIES USING PROVEN FINANCING STRATEGIES
+ BUILD WEALTH THROUGH FIX-AND-FLIP AND THE
BRRRR STRATEGY

FRANK EBERSTADT

TABLE OF CONTENTS

THE ULTIMATE REAL ESTATE INVESTING BEGINNER'S BOOK

Part III

PROFIT AND PROSPER

THE ULTIMATE HOUSE FLIPPING AND BRRRR REAL ESTATE INVESTING BEGINNER'S BOOK

Part I
LEARN THE STRATEGIES

Part II
TAKE ACTION AND MAKE SMART MOVES

Part III
BUILD SMART AND GROW BIG

THE ULTIMATE REAL ESTATE INVESTING BEGINNER'S BOOK

ACHIEVE FINANCIAL FREEDOM WITH RENTAL PROPERTIES USING PROVEN FINANCING STRATEGIES AND WEALTH-BUILDING TECHNIQUES

INTRODUCTION

When you think about real estate investing or simply purchasing a property, it can seem like something only rich people do. However, this is definitely not the case, and one man's story highlights this. Shaun Conlon was a pretty average guy from Ireland. He came from humble beginnings and decided to move to Chicago to earn some money. He started working as an assistant janitor, which didn't pay much. He painted apartments at night to make some more money and kept up with his routine for a few years. He saved up as much money as he could and bought an apartment after a few years. He then sold his apartment and made a profit, which was highly motivating for him. He got a taste of real estate investing and decided that this was what he wanted to do. He kept his job, but he invested in real estate and began selling real estate as a side job. He did this for over three years and became a top real estate broker. Then, he landed his first job at a brokerage and continued to hone his skills. About four years later, he was able to open his own real estate investment firm. He now uses real estate as his primary source of income, and it all started from a humble beginning.

"I was an ordinary person who did some fairly extraordinary things. It's America. You can still do those things."

— SEAN CONLON

The story simply highlights that anyone can get involved in real estate investing. It doesn't matter if you have tons of money to play with or just a few dollars in your piggy bank. There are strategies and ways in which you can dip your toes in the wonderful pool of real estate. Before moving on, it is important to understand what real estate investing is in the first place. When you invest in real estate, you are essentially investing in properties. You are using real estate as an investment vehicle to gain profit. There are many ways to generate a profit through real estate, and throughout this book, we will dive into each one of these methods and topics so you can fully understand how diverse real estate can be.

The two major categories of real estate are residential and commercial. Residential real estate is the type of property people live in, and commercial real estate is typically used to generate income on a larger scale. We are going to dive more into these two types of real estate, and many others, in the first chapter of this book. Real estate is multifaceted, and it's important to understand all the different types of real estate as well as all the ways you can invest. The reason anyone can invest in real estate is that there are so many options out there. You can tailor your investment strategy to suit your needs and goals.

Another common concern that people may have about investing in real estate is that it seems too risky. Property is expensive, and if you're putting a lot of money into something, you want to have a guaranteed positive outcome. I would love to say that you are guaranteed to make a lot of money through real estate, but we must realize that any kind of investing comes with its own level of risk. That being said, real estate tends to be one of the most stable forms of investment since property has a trend of increasing in value over time. Now, there are a few things that you have to consider, such as the location, amenities, and type of property, but this rule rings true if you do your research and choose the right property to invest in.

You don't have to be a homeowner first or choose the perfect time in the market to start investing in real estate. Your property investment journey can start right now, and it can be fruitful and rewarding. In fact, the longer you take, the more you delay the potential benefits of real estate investing. While there may be many excuses that you can make to not take the plunge into real estate investing, it simply means that you are delaying your potential wealth-building. Real estate is a cornerstone element for building your wealth, and it's a tool you can use to help reach your financial goals and additional stability in your life and future.

By the end of this book, you should have all the tools, tricks, and knowledge you need to confidently invest in real estate. The goal is to give you a comprehensive understanding of real estate investing as well as practical and actionable steps. This book is not just theory; there are also actions that you can take to help push you toward the right real estate investments. Interactive learning tools have been incorporated throughout the book to assist you with grasping concepts and give you practical aid along your real estate investment journey. All of this will help you have confidence in your decision-making so you can forge a path to financial freedom.

This book has been designed on a three-part framework. This way, you can first build a foundation and then work your way up into other aspects of real estate investing. The first part is going to be building the base. This essentially means that you will be building a firm foundation for your real estate knowledge. In this part, there are two chapters, and the overarching topics discussed will be the types of real estate investing and how to finance your real estate investments. Part two is about mastering the fundamentals and has three chapters within it. These three chapters cover the metrics of valuation, risk assessment, and actually purchasing your property. Finally, we have part three, which is about making a profit and prospering on your real estate journey. In this phase, there are five chapters, and the topics covered are tax benefits and legal considerations, passive income, short-term rentals, long-term success, and wealth building.

All of these parts are essential to investing successfully in real estate. They will give you all the knowledge you need to walk into your real estate investment journey with full confidence. By the end of this book, you should be well-equipped and ready to go. So many people wish they had started their real estate investment journey earlier in their lives. Regardless of your current life situation or your financial standing, you are in a good position to start investing in real estate. Simply picking up this book and taking the first step in the process already puts you on the right path. This is exactly where you need to be to find success when investing in real estate.

I have guided people through the process, and none has ever regretted it. Investing in real estate is one of the most fulfilling, exciting, and rewarding journeys you will ever go on. You don't have to make all the mistakes other people make because you now have the handbook and the directions away from all the pitfalls. I have already written books on Airbnb and how to use short-term rentals to build wealth. I have done it myself and, through these best-sellers, have guided others along the process. If you are interested, you can add to the knowledge from this book with guidance from my other books. This could be essential reading should you want to become an Airbnb host. Here are the titles:

- *How to Set Up and Run a Successful Airbnb Business:* Outearn Your Competition with Skyrocketing Rental Income and Leave Your 9 to 5 Job Even if You Are an Absolute Beginner
- *How to Unleash Your Airbnb's Full Potential: The Complete Step-By-Step Guide to Maximizing Bookings, Rental Income, Setting Up Automation and Optimizations for Your Short-Term Rental Business*

If you have ever wanted to invest in real estate but were unsure how to do it, you are in the right place. From here, we will build the base with Chapter 1 so you can fully understand the different types of real estate investing out there. Next, we are going to move on to two different topics that will build a robust framework for you to continue on your real estate investment journey. So, without further delay, let's jump into the first chapter.

PART I

BUILD A BASE

TYPES OF REAL ESTATE INVESTING

Ninety percent of all millionaires invest in some form of real estate (Red Oak, 2022). This is an incredibly high number and demonstrates that real estate is a viable option for building wealth and creating financial security. If nine out of ten millionaires choose to add real estate to their investment portfolio, then this is something that a beginner investor or somebody looking to build wealth should also look into. It is clear that real estate is a fantastically valuable asset in your overall investing portfolio.

An individual investor can invest in many types of real estate. This makes real estate investing even more attractive because you can find a type of real estate investment that is going to fit you and your goals perfectly. In order to make the right decision, it is important to understand the different types of real estate that you can invest in.

RESIDENTIAL REAL ESTATE

The first type of real estate we are going to be talking about is called residential real estate. This is one of the most popular types of real estate investments since it is accessible to the average person. On top of that, any person who has purchased a property, rented, or is in the housing market would have some experience with residential real estate, making it much easier to transition into this investment vehicle. Under the umbrella of residential real estate, you can purchase different kinds of properties, and each has its benefits and things to consider before investing.

Single-Family Homes

When it comes to residential properties, a single-family home is definitely one of the most popular and most common varieties out there. Not only are plenty of single-family homes currently on the market but there are also many constantly under development. This means there will be even more being brought onto the market. As the name implies, a single-family home is designed to meet the needs of a family. There are many varieties of properties that can fall under the category of a single-family home, and these include freestanding homes, cottages, villas, and even mansions.

These types of properties are incredibly popular with couples who have a family or are looking to establish a family. The reason for this is that there are key features in a single-family home that benefit the traditional family lifestyle. This includes having a garden, yard, or outdoor space for kids to play or adults to use for recreational and outdoor activities. These types of properties, specifically detached homes, also offer privacy because the home-owner would not be sharing space or walls with neighbors. The other benefit is that the homeowner has almost complete control over what they do with their property and can design and change things up as they see fit.

Multi-Family Homes

A multi-family home is more like an apartment or a duplex. With these types of properties, the people living within it will be sharing space and walls with their neighbors. From an investment stand-point, purchasing a multi-family home could be a good option because you can have multiple renters in one property, which means you are collecting multiple streams of rental income. Something that investors are doing with multi-family homes is called house hacking. This is when you stay in a portion of the property and then rent out the rest to a tenant. The tenant contributes to or covers the entire cost of the mortgage payment, which means you, as the investor, get to stay on the property for a fraction of the cost or completely for free.

Multi-family homes have a different target audience than single-family homes. Since there are communal living spaces such as gardens, lounges, and other areas, it may not be as attractive for larger families. These properties can be quite convenient to stay in, as many multi-family homes or apartments are close to city centers.

Condos

A condo or condominium is very similar to an apartment or a multifamily home, but these are typically situated in a larger building. Condos often offer more space than apartments and come with distinct ownership; each condo unit is individually owned, while apartments are usually rented. These types of properties have some shared amenities, but they do offer individuality, which means they are a blend of single-family and multi-family homes. There is a sense of community since many of the living spaces are shared, and you live in close proximity to your neighbors. On top of that, most condominiums are in desirable areas such as urban centers and cultural hubs, meaning the location is advantageous to many people, which can bring up the property's price.

Townhouses

With a townhouse, you are looking at a semi-standalone building attached to a collection of other houses or buildings. In many cases, a townhouse will offer a small yard, and you can think of a townhouse as a smaller version of a single-family home. There will be some shared amenities if the complex has a pool or communal gathering area. However, everything else is more private.

Sometimes, a townhouse will share a wall with a neighbor but offer the separation of a standalone house. These properties tend to be more affordable because they are smaller than single-family homes and are usually lower maintenance.

Mobile Homes

When considering investing in property, a mobile home may not be the first thing that comes to mind, but it is definitely an option. A mobile home is essentially a living space that is movable. To move these types of homes, you need to attach them to a specialized trailer or truck. It will have wheels so it is easily movable from place to place. It is also important to consider that a mobile home is designed differently, so you must understand the ins and outs of your particular mobile home to know how to move it and take care of it.

A mobile home is definitely more affordable than other real estate options, and it offers the flexibility of moving from place to place. These days, you can get some pretty advanced mobile homes with different rooms and living spaces that offer a lifestyle similar to that of a traditional home. There is also the option of permanently placing a mobile home on a support system that will act as a foundation. To do this, you need to rent or purchase the land on which you place the mobile home.

COMMERCIAL REAL ESTATE

The next category of real estate investment property is commercial real estate. For a property to fall under the category, it needs to generate profit through rental income or capital gains. It typically does not include properties that people live in from day to day.

Retail Spaces

The first category of commercial real estate is retail spaces. If you go to a shopping mall, you will see many stores, and the shop owners have to rent out these rooms or spaces in order to sell their products there. A restaurant or any other business that you might find in a shopping mall is also located in a retail space. There are also retail spaces that are a lot bigger and standalone. For example, if you visit a huge store like a Walmart or Costco, it may be a big center that stands alone without other stores around it. These still count as retail spaces.

Office Spaces

Offices are another option for commercial real estate buildings. This still generates income, even though there is no direct buying and selling of items from the office space. These spaces may be small suburban office buildings where only one company works or an office park where multiple companies rent the spaces. From an investor's point of view, these types of properties can be a lot more expensive to purchase, as an office building is quite a large investment but also generates a large amount of profit.

Industrial Properties

An industrial property is typically located outside an urban or suburban area. These types of properties are used for manufacturing, assembly, warehousing, and a mixture of all of these. These types of buildings need to be customized for the type of operations that will be running within them. Industrial property needs to be quite large because of the nature of the work occurring within the property. Some special licenses and permits may be needed for an industrial property due to the type of activity that is taking place.

Hotels and Motels

Even though people stay in hotels and motels, they are still categorized as commercial property. This is because they provide a service, and there may also be restaurants, boutiques, and shops within it. There are many different types of hotels and leisure properties out there. These could include ones that are full service, which means there is room service and a restaurant on site, whereas limited service means it is likely just going to provide the room for the guest to stay and may not have room service or a restaurant on site. There could also be extended stay rooms or options, such as an area equipped with a kitchen so guests can stay for longer periods. Resorts are also in this category, and they offer both full service and a large amount of land where people can take part in many recreational activities.

REAL ESTATE INVESTMENT TRUSTS (REITS)

A real estate investment trust is a great option for those who are looking to dip their toes into the water of real estate investment. The truth is that many forms of real estate investment come with a hefty price tag. It can take months or even years to save up enough to invest in real estate or build up your credit so that you can take out a loan to invest. A REIT helps you invest in real estate without having access to a large amount of funds. On top of that, you don't have to physically buy or manage property in order to invest.

The aim of a real estate investment trust is to create a liquid investment out of an illiquid asset. A REIT will combine the contributions from multiple investors to invest in property. Then, the profit from these investments will be shared among all who have contributed. REIT can invest in various kinds of properties, including complexes, townhouses, hotels, infrastructure, office buildings, shopping centers, warehouses, and residential real estate. This means an investor can diversify their real estate investment portfolio by simply investing in one thing. On top of that, investors do not have to put a lot of money into getting started with real estate investing. This makes real estate investing a lot more accessible and allows you to invest and get used to the real estate market as soon as possible. Since this type of invest-ment is managed by somebody else, not all your money will be invested in real estate. Some of your money will be put toward a fee for the management of your investment.

There are three main types of REITs: equity, mortgage, and hybrid. Equity REITs are the most common and are equity-based, meaning that revenues are typically brought in through rent charged to tenants. Mortgage REITs will lend money to property owners through loans or invest in mortgage-backed securities.

Revenue is primarily generated from the interest earned on these loans and securities. Finally, hybrid REITs mix both of the above strategies into one portfolio.

DEVELOPMENT AND LAND INVESTING

Investing in land means purchasing the raw land that property can be built upon or used for other purposes to generate revenue. There are many types of land investing out there, so interested investors should understand what they want to do with it and what type of investment they are trying to make. Regardless of how you choose to use the land, if it's an investment, you must choose the right location. A terrible location will not have much value and will, therefore, be a poor investment.

Whether the location is good or bad depends on what you will use the land for. If you want to build a house on the land, then you need to choose a location that is convenient and close to everyday amenities that the average family would need. If you want to build a warehouse or some sort of commercial property, you need to ensure that the land you purchase is an ideal location. For example, if you are looking to use the land for commercial purposes, you need to ensure that it is easy to get to so that people can either shop, live, work, or participate in recreational activities there. Other uses for the land could be farming practices, such as raising livestock or growing crops.

It is also possible to purchase a piece of land and not do anything with it besides basic upkeep and then sell it for a higher price later on down the line. Land appreciates in value, so it will continue to increase in value, especially if it is in a good location. If you are planning to build on the property, then it's important to budget accordingly. Building a house or other type of real estate costs a lot of money, and it also means that you will need to get the right people on board to help develop that land. It can also take quite a long time because you will need approval and paperwork in order to get started. This is why purchasing land to start a development may not be the best option for a beginner investor or somebody who wants to see their returns as soon as possible. However, if done correctly, this can be one of the best ways to make a large return on your investment.

HOUSE FLIPPING

House flipping is getting more popular, and for good reason. The goal of flipping a house is to purchase a property, renovate it, and then sell it as quickly as possible for a higher price than you bought it for. When trying to make the most profit from this, many investors choose to purchase undervalued properties. The property may not have been taken care of, or there might be something wrong with it that has caused it to drop in value. The investor will purchase the property and make the necessary repairs to bring the property price back up. The newly refurbished property can be sold for more, and the investor makes a profit in a short amount of time.

When investing in this way, it is important to research and ensure you understand the property you are purchasing. If there is too much damage or the renovations are going to cost you a lot of money, then it's not going to be worth purchasing. Any renovation or additional cost needs to be less than the potential profit you could make from selling the house. The positives to taking part in this type of real estate investment are that you get to diversify your real estate investment portfolio and have an investment with a quick turnaround time. When it comes to real estate investments, few options offer you a quick turnaround time so that you can get your profit soon after investing.

While flipping a house could be a wonderful addition to your investment portfolio, you also have to take into consideration that it is a risk. The goal of flipping a house is to sell it quickly, but there are no guarantees. You will be taking a risk of some financial loss or having to hold the property for longer than you might expect. You will also need to do your due diligence in terms of research when it comes to the renovations, as you need to make sure that you have enough finances available for the renovation costs. It is always a good idea to plan to spend more money than you think you'll need, as there may be unexpected costs along the way. Planning is always key in any kind of real estate investment, and flipping is no exception.

BUY, REHAB, RENT, REFINANCE, REPEAT (BRRRR)

While this acronym might be funny to say, this is a very legitimate method in real estate investing. It follows a very similar principle to house flipping, as you will purchase a distressed property and then rehab it to make a profit. However, instead of selling the property, you will rent it out. From here, you will then refinance the property by taking a cash-out refinance. With this money, you will buy other properties that need to be refurbished and rented out. The great thing about this method is that you use little of your money to invest. You are using the money from the refinancing to purchase a new property, and since you are renting out your properties, you are constantly making an income.

The goal is to build on the momentum and continue to repeat the process so that you can build a robust real estate portfolio. There are definitely risks when it comes to this method, as investing in a distressed property may not always be as easy as we would like. There could be damages and issues with the property that you cannot see at first glance, so you must get a professional to inspect the property before you make a purchase. This way, you are completely aware of what needs to be done and whether it's going to be worth it for you to purchase the property. You should also consider any legal limitations that specific areas or properties might impose for certain types of renovations or changes. Having a legal professional on your team is really going to help you and save you a lot of time and money. However, if you can find a good property to get started, then you can continue building on this and bring in a satisfying amount of income through this investment method.

VACATION RENTAL PROPERTIES

With the rise of vacation rental websites, such as Airbnb, it has become a lot easier for people to market their vacation or short-term rentals to the public. This can make you a lot of money if you are willing to open up your property to tourists and travelers. When you rent out your property as a vacation rental, it is essentially private accommodation for a short-term stay. It differs from a hotel, and you can decide what kinds of amenities you offer to your guests. Since this is a short-term rental property, it needs to be fully furnished so that people can have a comfortable stay. On top of that, you will need to ensure that you are giving your guests an enjoyable experience because they can rate your property and the service they get on many of the vacation rental websites. You must maintain an excellent reputation because word-of-mouth is a great marketing technique, and you want people to talk positively to their friends and family so you can get more bookings.

When it comes to a vacation or short-term rental, knowing what you are offering is important. Location is also really important, as you need to have a property somewhere where people actually want to stay—for example, a cottage on the beach or an apartment in a big city. If you have a property close to any popular tourist destination, then you are already a suitable candidate to have a vacation rental. If you want to purchase a property as a short-term rental, then make sure you choose the right location and pick somewhere where people will travel and want to stay.

Since there are people in and out of your property, you can make more money than if you rented out the property on a long-term basis. You could have multiple tenants or guests within a month and make a huge profit. With this being said, it is important to consider that there will be periods when people are not as willing to vacation or travel. For example, during the summer months, vacation homes and vacation rentals will be more popular since more people are traveling. However, when it gets to the colder months or when work tends to pick up, such as the financial year-end, it may be a low season when people are not traveling as much. In these seasons, you may not make a lot of money.

Another thing that you need to consider is higher maintenance requirements when it comes to vacation rentals since multiple people use the space. It is also your responsibility to ensure that the space is safe. Short-term rentals also mean having to turn around the property for your new guests so it is clean and ready for their stay. This means it is not a completely passive form of income since you will need to actively check up on the property, ensure your guests are fine, and make sure that the property is up to scratch for each one of your guests when they check in. If there are complaints or emergencies from your guests, then you will need to rush to their side in order to assist them. If you do not have the time to take care of a short-term rental, you can hire a property management company to do it for you. This does come at a cost, but it may be worth it since you do not have to handle the day-to-day running of the property. This is also a good option if you have multiple rental properties you are trying to manage.

INTERACTIVE ELEMENT: WORKSHEET TO DETERMINE PERSONAL INVESTMENT PREFERENCES

Asking the right questions is essential when determining your investment goals and preferences. Go through this worksheet to help you understand your preferences and investment style. Remember to answer the questions honestly.

Scan the QR code to download a printable version of all interactive elements.

What is your primary goal when it comes to real estate investing?

_____

How much money do you aim to use as an initial investment?

_____

How comfortable are you with high-risk investments that can potentially lead to higher returns?

_____

Do you prefer:

1) A stable, lower-risk property with modest returns.

2) A higher-risk property with high earning potential.

_____

Would you prefer to hire a property manager or take a more do-it-yourself approach?

_____

List the properties discussed in this chapter in order of what interests you most to least.

_____

_____

_____

There are many types of real estate you can invest in, and this is a good thing. You get to choose the types that best suit your needs and speak to you the most. This is an important decision, so take some time to think about it. We discussed the different ways you can invest in real estate and the strategies you can use. As a beginner, choosing one to focus on is best; from there, you can grow your investment portfolio.

Now that you have a clearer picture of the various real estate investment options and have assessed your personal preferences, it's time to explore how to finance these investments.

2

FINANCING YOUR INVESTMENTS

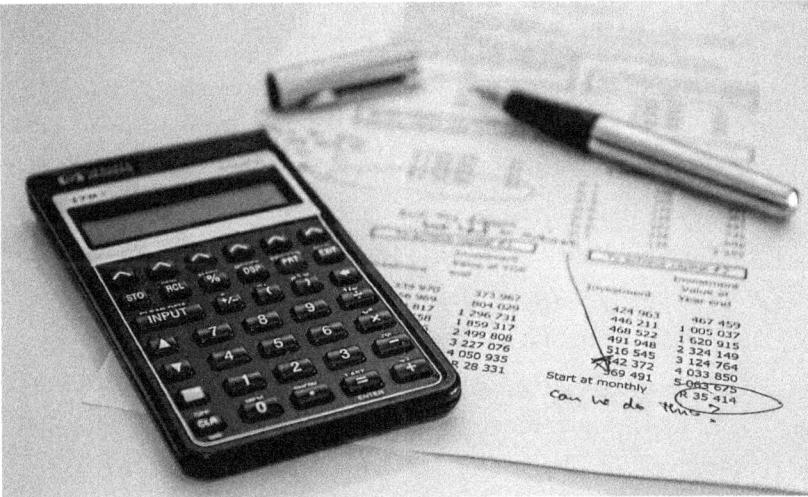

W hen it comes to investing in real estate, over 80 percent of buyers finance their investments (National Association of Realtors, 2018). This means that most people who own property or invest in real estate are not buying with cash but rather financing their investments. Financing means borrowing money from someone else, often a financial entity, in order to have the funds to make your investment. There are many ways to do this, so in this chapter, we will dive deeper into the topic.

FINANCING KEY TERMS

- **Interest Rate:** This is a percentage fee placed on a loan's principal amount.
- **Principal:** The amount borrowed without the addition of any interest.
- **Amortization:** A method of accounting used to distribute or spread loan payments over a specified period of time, in which each payment covers both principal and interest.
- **Loan-to-Value:** This is a ratio that is worked out by taking the loan amount and dividing it by the asset purchased or any collateral being borrowed against.
- **Lenders Mortgage Insurance:** A type of insurance that protects the lender. As the investor, you need to pay if you are borrowing over 80 percent of the value of the property you want to purchase.
- **Collateral:** A way to secure a loan is by pledging an asset, so if you default on the loan and cannot pay it back, the lender can take that asset to recuperate the money you owe them.
- **APR:** This stands for the annual percentage rate and is the yearly cost of a loan. This will include all charges, fees, and interest rates.

There are many different financing options available. This is a good thing because it means you'll be able to find an option that works best for you. Since every investor is different and has different strategies and a different amount of money, it is important to choose the financing option that is going to suit your needs the best.

Traditional Loans

The most common way to finance a property is through a traditional loan. There are a few different types of traditional loans, and you must consider the service provider. Each financial service provider will have their own terms and rules surrounding specific loans, so it is important to not only understand the type of loan you're taking out but also compare different service providers.

Fixed-Rate Mortgages

When the term fixed is used in financing, it means that there will be no change or movement. A fixed rate means there is a fixed interest rate for the entire duration of the loan. This interest rate is agreed upon prior to the loan being taken out, and it stays the same until you have paid off the loan in full or the loan term has ended. Many people choose this type of mortgage because the interest rate does not fluctuate with what is happening in the market. Since a mortgage or a home loan is a significant commitment that spans many years, having a fixed rate means more security and predictability.

Variable-Rate Mortgages

Conversely to a fixed-rate mortgage, a variable-rate mortgage has a monthly repayment that can change because the interest rate can change. This means it can either go up or down, and you pay either more or less. The benefit of this type of mortgage is that it allows you to overpay on your payments, which means you could potentially pay off your mortgage much more quickly. For example, if the rate moves to a lower percentage than what you usually pay, you could make your usual payment, meaning that you are paying over the required amount. This money is not lost but put toward your principal, helping you pay off your mortgage sooner.

The downside to this type of mortgage is that your payments will change over time. This will definitely affect how you budget and plan your future finances. You are also risking a higher interest rate than what you might have originally planned due to an uncertain economic situation. At the end of the day, the economic markets are unpredictable.

Interest-Only Loan/Mortgage

This type of mortgage is set up quite differently from the ones we have already discussed. With an interest-only mortgage, the borrower will only pay the interest required on the loan for a specified period of time. Once this time has elapsed, the borrower will owe the principal amount in a lump sum or based on an agreed-upon payment schedule. With other types of mortgages and home loans, you must repay the principal and the interest in your monthly repayments.

The benefit of this type of home loan is that you will pay back a minimal amount each month for the beginning portion of the mortgage term. This will help if you need some additional cash flow and expect your income to increase over the next few years. It may also be a good option for investors who are looking to flip the property or gain an income from the property in the coming years. This way, they are deferring larger payments to focus on their investments. However, it is a risk because you never know how finances are going to play out in the future, and once the interest-only portion of the mortgage term has ended, you will then be required to pay back the principal, and this means the overall monthly repayments are going to be much higher.

Balloon Mortgages

With a balloon mortgage, you will be required to make small payments for a certain period at the beginning of your loan term. This is followed by one large balloon payment once the term has ended. When taking out this type of mortgage, it is important to ensure that you will be able to afford the balloon payment at the end of the term. This type of mortgage can be tempting because the repayments are so low at the beginning. However, if you are not fully prepared to pay the balloon amount at the end of the mortgage term, it could result in you falling into a lot of debt, so ensuring that you have a plan in place is key if you are considering this type of mortgage.

Lease Options and Rent-to-Own

Let's first talk about a lease option, which is where you enter into an agreement with the current property owner to lease the property for a certain amount of time with the option to purchase it later down the line. This means that you have the opportunity to purchase the property once the lease is over. To have the chance to purchase the property, you, as the renter, will need to pay something called an "option fee upfront." This fee is included in your monthly rent and will also go toward the down payment of the property. This is not any kind of agreement to purchase the property, so the renter is not obligated to make the purchase after the lease has ended.

A rent-to-own agreement is exactly the same as a lease option but with a slightly different name. There is no obligation to purchase the house after the lease expires, but the current property owner can only sell after first giving you the option to purchase it as the renter. If the agreement is a lease-purchase contract, then you are required to purchase the property once the lease comes to an end.

This option is good for those who are trying to save up for a bigger down payment or simply do not have the funds to purchase the house outright and would like to rent first. Once the lease ends, the renter is required to purchase the property.

Seller Financing

With a traditional mortgage, you must go to a financial service provider and apply for the loan. The service provider will pay for your mortgage, and you will pay them back in monthly installments. An alternative to this financing method is called seller financing. With this method, the seller of the property will act as the mortgage lender. All this means is that there is no intermediary, and you will pay your mortgage installments directly to the person selling the property. This is a unique situation, and you will need to find a seller who is willing to enter into this kind of financing agreement. If you find somebody willing, you get to skip a lot of the red tape associated with getting a mortgage and can handle all transactions directly with the seller of the property. In this case, the seller will set out the mortgage and down payment terms. You may also be able to negotiate better if you are doing it directly with the seller of the property.

Cash-Out Financing

If you are looking for a way to access the equity that is currently sitting in your properties, then a cash-out refinance could be a good option for you. Essentially, when you apply for a cash-out financing option, you are replacing the mortgage you have at that moment with a larger loan, and the difference is given to you in a lump-sum payment. You can choose to use this money however you would like, but from an investment point of view, most investors will use it to invest in other properties or their current property to increase its value. The rules for this type of financing will vary based on where you are and the financial service provider you decide to go with, but in most cases, you will need at least 20 percent equity in your home. This means you would have needed to pay off at least 20 percent of what you owe on the property before considering a cash-out financing option. It is also a good idea to ensure that the interest rate you are getting on the new loan is not much more than what you are currently paying; otherwise, this could be a bad financial move. These types of loans should only be taken out if you have a plan in place and know what you're going to do with the money.

Home Equity Line of Credit (HELOCs)

With this financing option, you can cash in on the equity you currently have on your property through variable-rate financing. HELOC is a revolving line of credit that works similarly to a credit card. When you take out this line of credit, you do not have to use it if you do not need it. You are free to borrow the money you need and repay it as you use it or whenever you choose to pay it back. Most people will use this type of financing to make improvements to their homes or other aspects of their property investments. It basically just gives you access to additional funds so that you can spend it in other areas.

GETTING PREPARED FOR FINANCING

The process of receiving financing for your property investments doesn't start when you are ready to make the purchase. It starts as early as possible in your life because having a good financial standing is incredibly important. You can prepare yourself for big purchases from the time you start earning your own money and building up your credit score.

Improving Your Credit Score

Your credit score is extremely important when it comes to making any kind of big purchase and getting a loan from a financial institution. The bank or other financial service providers will look at your credit score to determine whether or not you are responsible with your money and if they can trust you with a big loan. It is a risk for financial service providers to give out big loans at good interest rates, which is why they look at the credit score to mitigate this risk. When you have a good credit score, it's a lot easier for you to get financing. You will get a good interest rate and terms on your loan so that you do not have to pay more than you need to. You also have more financing options, so you don't have to go with whichever provider offers you any kind of loan.

You can check your credit score on any of the major credit bureaus, and this is completely free. Depending on how well you have managed your credit over the past few years, you will either have a good or bad credit score. A good credit score is typically over 620; anything lower can be considered bad or moderate. The goal is to get your credit score as high as possible so you can give yourself the best opportunity for your mortgage. It is always best to start off on the right foot with building your credit score, but if you have a lower credit score, you can also work to build it up. The tips we will talk about in this section will help you build your credit score from scratch or increase a low credit score.

The first thing you need to do is have a look at all of your bills and make sure you know when they need to be paid each month. Missing bill payments or paying them late has a negative impact on your credit score. If you have any debit orders, you also need to make sure there is money in your account when your debit orders are taken to ensure you are not missing those payments. It's helpful to move all your payment dates to the same day or week so it's easy for you to remember to pay them.

The next thing you need to do is look at all your credit card balances to see how much you owe on your credit cards. Then, you will need to work on reducing these balances as much as possible. Owing too much money on a credit card negatively affects your credit score. You should only use about 20 to 30 percent of your available credit at any time. This is a safe area to be in, but lowering it as much as possible will help you stay out of debt. This leads to the next point—making sure your credit utilization is also low. Credit utilization is how much of your available credit you are actually using, and when you keep it low, it shows that you can manage having this credit available.

While you are working toward building up your credit score, you must not add any additional debt. Try not to get any more credit cards or any additional loans. Building your credit score takes small steps. Every month is going to compound, and you will have a good credit score sooner if you stick to the plan.

Down Payment Requirements

An important thing to consider when you are looking into taking out a mortgage or other financing option for an investment property is your down payment. Most types of financing will require you to have a down payment ready. On top of that, the larger the down payment you have available, the smaller the mortgage loan you will need for your investment. In general, it is better to have a larger down payment, especially if this is your first investment. Typically, there is a 15 percent required down payment for most types of property financing, but it is advisable to save 20 to 30 percent of the property price as a down payment.

There are also some other requirements you should aim to hit before you start applying for mortgages and home loans. For example, having a credit score above 680 is going to be in your favor. If you can get it higher than this, you will put yourself in an even better position. You also want to make sure that your debt-income ratio is lower than 50 percent. This means that you are making twice as much as you owe on your debts. This just gives security to lenders, showing that you have the finances available to pay off your debts.

If you haven't started saving toward an emergency fund, this is a good time to start because having about six months' worth of reserve finances is essential in life. This is going to help protect your finances if unexpected situations occur in your life. On top of that, having these reserve finances shows lenders you are financially responsible and have finances available should you not have access to your salary or if there's some other unexpected emergency that needs to be taken care of. All these aspects play important roles when getting a home loan, as well as being able to manage one when you have it.

Saving for Your Down Payment

There are a few things that you can do to help yourself when you are saving for a down payment. This will take some sacrifice, but it will definitely be worth it when you can afford the property you really want to invest in. The first step when saving toward anything is to budget and cut down on unnecessary expenses. Most of us do not really know how much we are spending until we write it down and create a budget, and when you do this, it'll be a lot easier for you to see where your money is going and where you need to cut back. A budget will help you plan your finances in every area of your life.

Saving is incredibly important. There is only so much you are going to be able to save since you need to use your money for your daily expenses. Looking for ways to increase your income is essential when you are saving toward bigger purchases or any kind of financial goal. This way, you can create more revenue for yourself to work with, and you can save quickly. When it comes to saving, it is also important that you make it a priority. You can do this by creating an automatic transfer from your main account into your savings account. This way, you don't even have to think about saving; it is just done for you.

When you are saving toward a goal, it is important that you track your savings and see how you are progressing toward it. This will allow you to pick up on any potential saving pitfalls to resolve the issue as quickly as possible and get yourself back on track. You will also be able to recognize whether you are on track for your saving goals, and if you are not, then you can make a plan to adjust your current spending habits to align more with your goals. This is an excellent way to ensure that you put yourself in the best position to save money and reach your financial goals.

INTERACTIVE ELEMENT: CALCULATE YOUR LOAN-TO-VALUE RATIO

Loan-to-value is an important calculation to figure out if an investment will be a good choice or not. You can use this simple formula to work it out:

LTV% = (Loan Amount / Asset Value) x 100

When calculating your LTV, aim for a lower ratio. Lenders typically view lower LTVs more favorably, as they signify reduced financial risk for them. A lower LTV often results in better financing options, including lower interest rates, especially when the ratio is at or below 80%. However, achieving a lower LTV may require a larger down payment on your part.

You can fill out this worksheet to compare different properties and determine which will be the best investments.

LTV%	Loan Amount	Asset Value
35%	$140,000	$400,000

Financing is one of the most important things to think about when it comes to real estate investing. Since property is such an expensive asset, choosing the right type of financing could save you a lot of money or end up costing you in the end. It is always best to start preparing yourself as early as possible. In fact, you can start now, even before you have an investment in mind. With a solid grasp of financing options, it's time to go deeper into evaluating real estate investments. Next is Part 2 of our framework: Master the Fundamentals.

PART II

MASTER THE
FUNDAMENTALS

UNDERSTANDING KEY METRICS

Alex became an accidental landlord very early on in his life. By the time he was twenty-five, both his parents had passed away, and they left him with a condo in California. He didn't really know much about property investment and actually thought about selling the condo quite a few times. However, he decided to keep it even though he didn't even live in California. He hired a property management company to handle the day-to-day business since he could not do it himself. It didn't make him that much profit, but it wasn't a liability at that stage either. You could say that he almost completely forgot about it, but it gave him a little insight into property management and what it entailed.

Over the next few years, he prioritized saving toward his retirement and building up a good portfolio for his future. However, these investments were not making as steady progress as he would've liked. This led him to think about other options. One day, he remembered his condo in California, and even though it wasn't making him a great profit, he recognized that property could be a wonderful investment. This is when he started doing more research. He figured out why his property wasn't making that much and decided to fix some of the issues—or at least not make the same mistakes with his next investment. For example, he knew California was a very expensive state and that the rent you could charge was really not worth it, based on the expenses needed to run a rental. With this information, he decided to invest in property in cheaper states, which would help him turn a bigger profit. He also looked at properties that would appreciate in value, which meant purchasing properties at a cheaper price so he could increase the value and make more profit. He also ensured the properties he was looking to invest in had lower operating costs so he could maximize his potential profits.

Having a strategy in place really helped him to aggressively start investing and grow his real estate portfolio. With the strategy in place, it took him about four years, and suddenly, he owned thirty-five rentals that were bringing in a massive income. This was helping him to save toward his retirement and other financial goals, ensuring he and his family had financial security for the future. While it took him a while to realize the value of real estate, once he did, he was able to put a plan in place that really helped him to increase investment opportunities and make real estate a viable investment choice.

CASH FLOW

When it comes to investments or running a business, it is important to have cash flow. Speaking of cash flow, you'll notice that people refer to it as positive cash flow or negative cash flow. When you have a positive cash flow, it means that you have cash left after you have spent money on all of your expenses. It basically means that you are turning a profit. However, if you have a negative cash flow, it means that your expenses are more than what you are making. When you have negative cash flow, it means you don't have any money to continue to grow the business. It is highly important to ensure that you do everything you can to maintain a positive cash flow, as this will result in you having money to put into your investments and continue to grow your overall investment portfolio.

It is very easy to work out cash flow, and it is one of the most important numbers when it comes to your investments. It's a simple way to see whether you are making a profit and whether you will be able to pay your bills when it comes to your properties. If you have a negative cash flow, it indicates that you may be overspending in certain areas or that the investment you made is not viable. In some cases, you have a negative cash flow for one month, and then the next few months have a positive cash flow. Therefore, it is important to track your cash flow over the course of a few months so you can get a better idea of how your investments are performing.

When you have multiple properties in your real estate investment portfolio, it becomes even more important for you to track your cash flow. You will need the cash for the individual properties as well as the overall cash flow in your entire investment portfolio. Your overall cash flow will give you a snapshot of how your portfolio is performing, and cash flow for individual property investments shows you which ones are turning the most profit and which ones you will need to reevaluate. Cash flow is also an indicator of where you need to put in more work or effort to increase the profit of certain properties.

PROPERTY APPRECIATION

Property appreciation takes place when the value of a piece of real estate gradually increases over time. There are many reasons for the value increase, including the general real estate market, the economy, and improvements or renovations to the actual property. Appreciation is one of the fundamental ways many real estate investors make an income through their real estate investments. When investing in a property, the goal is to choose one with the best chance of appreciation.

In order to figure out whether a property is a good candidate for overall appreciation, you will need to look at a few key points. These are the market demand, economic indicators, and location. Market demand simply means that more people want to live in a certain area or purchase the property that you have. If there are more people who want to purchase properties in the area that you have invested in, the overall property prices will increase. You can gauge future market demand by looking at areas currently being developed and where other investors are choosing to put their money. As a first-time investor, you can also look at places that already have a high market demand to see if you can purchase any properties within or close to that area.

Economic indicators have a tremendous impact on all types of investments, and real estate is no exception. These economic indicators could be job growth or creation, interest rates, and inflation. If the economy is moving in a positive direction, the price of real estate will probably increase. However, in the case of an economic downturn, the price of property might decrease. It is important to understand that there are always highs and lows when it comes to the economy, so it will never be completely stable throughout the lifespan of your investments. However, you may be able to use it to your advantage if you do your research.

You could purchase properties when they are at a lower price, and then when the economy picks up again, these properties will appreciate in value and give you a larger profit.

Location is easily one of the most important aspects to consider when investing in property. People will pay a lot more money for a lot less if the location is good. We know this because properties in central hubs and big cities tend to be much more expensive to buy and rent than those on the outskirts or in inconvenient areas. You will probably pay double or triple the amount to buy an apartment in New York or London compared to what you would pay if you purchased a property of the same size in an outlying area. Location is so important because people want to live near employment opportunities, amenities, and safe neighborhoods and areas. This doesn't mean that you have to purchase properties in big cities, but you have to make sure that you are choosing the right location and that it is going to be somewhere where people want to live. Look for up-and-coming areas with good schools that are walkable, safe, and have all the necessary amenities nearby.

EQUITY

When we speak about equity, it simply represents how much of the property you actually own. It shows you how much money you would get from the property if you were to sell it immediately. To figure out your equity, you need to subtract the outstanding balance of your mortgage from the current market value of the property. If you sold the property immediately, you would need to pay off the mortgage before you could take any profit from it. This is why many investors do their best to pay off the mortgage as quickly as possible so they have more equity in their investments.

You can use or leverage equity in a way that is beneficial to your investments and overall profit. One way you can do this is by improving your property to increase the market value. Since the mortgage payments are already agreed upon and will not change, making improvements to the property to increase its value will not impact how much you owe on your mortgage but will impact how much the property is worth. When you sell the property, you will get a larger profit since the property is more valuable. You can make many types of home improvements, like adding new rooms and amenities and making the home more aesthetically pleasing.

You can also consider taking out a home equity loan, which allows you to get cash based on the equity of your current property. You will use that money to improve your current property or even invest in additional properties to continue growing your real estate investment portfolio. This needs to be done with caution, and you will need to ensure you do your research before taking out this type of loan. However, investments can increase your overall profit and make your investment portfolio more valuable.

NET OPERATING INCOME (NOI)

The net operating income is the income generated from operating your property after deducting operating expenses. This amount does not include your mortgage payments. However, it does include most other things that you will pay for when it comes to your property. This will include insurance, property management fees, maintenance, and property taxes. To figure it out, all you have to do is look at the total revenue your property is bringing in and measure it up to the total operating expenses. This is an important figure, especially if you are using your property to bring in some sort of income, for example, if you are renting out your property. However, if you are living in your property and not using it for any kind of current profit, then you do not need to work out NOI.

You never want to spend more money than you are making. If the net operating income is very low or is a negative amount, this is a good indication that you are either spending too much or charging too little. With this information, you will then change your strategy to either lower your expenses or increase the rent you are charging so you can make a good profit from your property. Remember that your total income is being considered when you are working this out, so ensure you include rental income and other sources of revenue that your properties are bringing in. This could be revenue from the use of amenities such as laundry machines or parking fees. You will then subtract the total expenses from your total revenue in order to get your net operating income.

CAP RATE

The cap rate, or capitalization rate, is the net operating income divided by the purchase price or current market value. This figure is calculated to help an investor measure the return on investment of a property. A cap rate helps investors estimate the return they may expect to generate on their investment property. It is important to recognize that this is not a set-in-stone number, and many things can affect a cap rate. This is simply a prediction or estimate that an investor can use when making decisions.

Many factors can affect a cap rate. These include location, the size of the property, market stability, growth potential, and capital liquidity. Many investors use a cap rate to compare potential investments and see which one will be the most profitable. They will take into account all the factors above and figure out which one of the potential property investments will be the most profitable for them. For example, imagine there are two properties that an investor has their eye on. They are very similar in every way, except they are in different geographical locations. The investor will need to take this into consideration. The geographical location affects the net operating income and the potential returns the property can make. One property could be in a remote location. That means profit will be lower. Operating expenses will also be lower. The property could be in a big city, but this means that the operating expenses will be more expensive, and the rent you can charge and the amount of money you can make through this property will be a lot more. From here, the investor can work out the cap rate to see which one is going to be more profitable and then decide which property to invest in. You can work out the cap rate with this formula.

Cap Rate = Net Operating Income / Current Market Value

INTERACTIVE ELEMENT: CALCULATE THE NOI FOR A SAMPLE PROPERTY

The best way to understand NOI is to do it yourself. This is easier than you may think. The first thing you need to do is work out how much your potential property will make. This includes rent and other income sources such as:

- Parking fees
- Cleaning fees—charges collected from guests or tenants for cleaning services
- Charges for amenities
- Vending machines
- Laundry

Next, you will need to determine how much the property's expenses will come to. Many expenses could come up; the most common are:

- Utilities
- Taxes
- Repair and maintenance
- Insurance
- Accounting fees
- Legal fees
- Property management fees
- Cleaning fees—costs paid by the landlord for cleaning services
- Marketing expenses

The next figure you will need is the Gross Operating Income. It can be worked out with this formula:

Gross Operating Income = Potential Rental Income – Vacancy Losses

After you have all three figures, you can plug them into this formula to find out the NOI of a property:

NOI = (Gross Operating Income + Other Income) – Operating Expenses

To practice this, you can choose a few properties currently listed for sale on a property website. Try to find out as much information about them as possible and follow the above steps to find out their NOIs. You can then compare to see the difference. You can use the template below.

Income

Name	Amount
Total	

Expenses

Name	Amount

Total	

After financial metrics, we now delve into property valuation and risk assessment. The next chapter helps you with these so you can make well-informed investment decisions.

PROPERTY VALUATION AND RISK ASSESSMENT

C amila decided she was ready to start on her real estate investment journey. She found a wonderful apartment that she believed she could rent out to bring in a significant income. The process was going smoothly, and she decided to make an offer on the property. While waiting for the final paperwork and the details to be finalized, she decided she wanted to get the property valuated by her property evaluation expert. Before this, she had simply trusted the seller on the value of the property. After a few days, her property evaluator came back to her and said that the property was valued at much less than she thought and much less than the offer she had put in.

She was quite surprised by this and went back to the seller to ask for clarification. The property owner was adamant that the original pricing was correct and that Camila's evaluator was the one who was wrong. Since Camilla had already made an offer, the property seller knew how much money was on the table and refused to bring down the price. After a few days of back-and-forth, Camilla was forced to let go of the property. This was a hard one for her because she really believed that this property would be the perfect investment. It took her six months to find another similar property that could offer her great investment benefits.

A lot goes into investing in real estate, and property valuation is one of the most important aspects. It's easy to look at a property and think it is valued at a certain amount, but once the property has been inspected, it could be a completely different result. Getting a property inspected will help to ensure that you are paying a fair amount for the property, and if you already own it, you will get a fair amount if you choose to sell it.

VALUATING PROPERTIES

Property valuation is simply the assessment that your property will undergo in order to determine its value based on various factors, including location, amenities, and size. Property valuation is an incredibly important step in any real estate process, not only for the people who are buying and selling but also for other aspects, such as property insurance and taxation.

During the property assessment, the property surveyor or inspector will look at all the space on the property. They will consider the condition, size, number of rooms, age, and any potential for future development of the property. It is highly important to get a reputable professional to do this so you can get an accurate property assessment. It is also a good idea to have your own property assessor look at a property that you are planning to buy. This will give you peace of mind and ensure you are not overpaying for a piece of real estate.

Home value can be broken up into three different categories. These are assessed value, fair market value, and appraised value. A tax assessor in your municipality determines the assessed value and is only used for tax purposes. If the value is high, then taxes will be high. Fair market value is the amount you would be expected to get if you sell your property. The appraised value is the price given to you after a professional appraisal has been done on the property and is a more accurate representation of the property's value and what the seller should expect to get for it.

CMA

CMA stands for comparative market analysis, and it is used to estimate a property's price based on similar properties recently sold in the same area. Real estate agents do this type of analysis and then give it to people who want to sell their properties so they're able to list at an appropriate price. Property buyers can also use this to make a competitive offer on a property they are interested in purchasing. While real estate agents use their own special tools to do this kind of analysis, you can also do a basic form of a CMA on your own. All you have to do is go onto property listing websites and see how much properties are going for, and this will give you a good idea of what you should expect to pay for a similar property or what you can expect other people to pay for a property that you are looking to sell.

You can expect a CMA report to include aspects such as location, size, square footage, age of the property, number of rooms and bedrooms, any special features, the date of the sale, and the terms of financing for the sale. If you're looking to do your own CMA, there are a few steps you'll need to go through to ensure it's as accurate as possible. First, you will need to have a look at the neighborhood and whether it is a pleasant neighborhood. A good neighborhood is typically identified through the amenities, cleanliness, safety, and proximity to transportation and other necessities.

Next, you have to look at the property and gather the relevant details. If you're looking to purchase a property, you can look at the online listing to get a general idea of what the property provides, but it is always best to do an in-person visit to ensure the listing details are accurate. When you do a visit, make sure that you look at the size of the home, style, age, condition, layout, and general livability of the space. You will then need to list three to five comparable properties in the same area. These properties should have been recently sold so you can get the closest comparison possible, as the price of real estate fluctuates quite quickly.

Once you have done this, you will need to adjust for any differences between the comparable properties you have used and the ones that you are interested in buying. Every property is going to have differences of some sort, so it is important to understand these and their monetary impact. Professionals have prices and values assigned to certain differences. For example, if the property you are looking to purchase has an extra bedroom compared to comparable properties, this will significantly impact the price, as an extra bedroom or bathroom adds value to a property.

CMAs are definitely not perfect, but they can give you a great idea of how much you should expect to pay if you purchase a property and how much you should expect to get if you were to sell your property. It allows you to plan and budget effectively before you make an offer or even start the purchasing process, ensuring you are not getting a bad deal when buying or selling your property. The CMA is essentially a base around which you can build your real estate investment pricing.

RISK ASSESSMENT

When it comes to investing in real estate, there will always be some risk involved. Typically, the more risk an investor is willing to endure, the higher the potential reward could come from the investment. With that being said, it is unwise to take risks without assessing the risk and seeing if the potential reward is actually going to be worth it. When we talk about risk, we're talking about losing the money that we have invested. When it comes to real estate, risk is more of a complicated topic because so many factors can play into a property's value. On top of the value, you also have to consider whether it would be easy to sell the property when the time comes or to rent it out to tenants.

When thinking about risk and how it affects real estate, there are several aspects to consider. The first aspect is the real estate market. We already know that this market is incredibly unpredictable, and while there are forecasts used for market prediction, in many cases, these are not completely accurate. When it comes to the market, things like supply, demand, government policies, and unforeseen national events can all play a huge part in the value of a property. It is a good idea to have a look at the market and see what the forecast is saying so that you can plan. Still, it is also important to recognize that unpredictability is the only thing that is predictable in the real estate market. With that being said, typically, the real estate market goes up over time, so even though there are pockets of time where the market will be in a downturn, it is highly likely that it will pick up again.

Structural risk is an important type of risk that must be considered when purchasing a property. Every property will have its flaws, but it is important to understand what these flaws are to make sure you are investing in something that will last for the long term and will not cost you a bundle to rectify. For example, something like a damaged foundation or mold within the building is going to cost you a lot of money to repair, and in some cases, it might be irreparable. However, smaller structural issues could be fixed and dealt with. Purchasing a property with some structural issues will probably be cheaper, but you have to consider the amount you will be paying to complete the repairs.

Location is easily one of the most important factors you need to consider when investing in any kind of real estate. With that being said, location can also be a risk factor, especially if the area is not good or goes downhill from the time that you purchased the property. It is highly important that you research the location before you make a purchase, as this will be one of the biggest factors to impact the value of your property.

Another risk factor to consider is liquidity and cash flow. When it comes to real estate, there is not a lot of liquidity available since all of your money is going to be tied up in the physical property. You won't be able to quickly pull out some money from your investment for an emergency or if you want to purchase something else. There is a long process to get your money out of a real estate investment, so it is important to understand that even though property increases your overall net worth, you might not have access to that money until much later on. Cash flow is another thing to consider, as a negative cash flow is an enormous risk to any investor. Ensuring you make the right investments and set yourself up for positive cash flow is essential. If you realize you are going through a period where you have a negative cash flow, it is important to figure out why this is so you can solve the problem before you lose too much money.

A huge factor when it comes to real estate investment is your tenants. If you rent out your property to other people, there will always be a risk that they will not pay or they will not take good care of the property. You can't control other people and what they do, but you can ensure you do your research beforehand and don't accept tenants simply because they have applied. There needs to be a screening process before you allow somebody to move into your property to ensure they will pay on time and take care of your property. If they don't, you will spend a lot of time, money, and effort trying to get your rent and fix any of the issues they may cause. In line with this, another risk is vacancies if you cannot find tenants for your property. If you have vacancies for long periods of time, it means that you are not making money, and your cash flow will go into the negative. There are many things that could cause vacancies, such as the economic market or the location of the property. In order to mitigate this, you will need to ensure that you have done your research to purchase a property that is in demand and that people will more likely want to stay in. You will also need to price your property competitively to attract more potential tenants. Marketing is also very important, and it may be worth it to get a real estate expert on board to assist you.

We always talk about how property tends to appreciate in value over time, but another risk is property depreciation. If the property loses value over time, it is depreciating in value. It is important to choose the property you are going to invest in very carefully. Researching real estate markets and statistics when it comes to the type of property and its location will help you ensure you are setting yourself up for success with your investment. It is also a good idea to monitor the market even when you already have a property you have invested in. If you notice a risk of depreciation, it may be worth it to consider selling to save yourself from losing a lot of money. When it comes to investing in real estate, it is not simply purchasing a property and leaving it there. You will need to constantly be doing market analysis to ensure that you mitigate any risks as early as possible.

INTERACTIVE ELEMENT: CALCULATE THE CAP RATE OF A PROPERTY

In order to get the CAP rate of a property, you will first need to have the NOI. In the previous chapter, you worked this out for a sample property. You can use those figures in this exercise as well. Here is the formula for the CAP rate:

Cap Rate = Net Operating Income / Property's Sale Price or Market Value

There is a lot that can go into defining what a good cap rate is. Typically, between 8 percent and 12 percent is good, but in some cases, lower than this is also favorable.

After valuation and risk assessment, you're now ready to move forward with purchasing a property.

5

PURCHASING THE PROPERTY

An interesting statistic is that 75 percent of recent homebuyers have regrets about their purchase (Zillow, 2022). This is a huge number, and it can make people wonder whether real estate is actually worth it if so many people regret it. The reason so many new homeowners tend to regret their purchase is that the property requires a lot more maintenance and work than they initially expected. Knowing this, it's clear that many people who purchase property do not do the research they need to. It is so important to do the relevant research before you make such a big purchase. This regret can definitely be avoided if people knew what they were getting into and were prepared for it from the start.

PREPARING TO BUY

Preparation is key when you are looking to make a large purchase, like when it comes to real estate. You definitely don't want to be part of the 75 percent of people who have regrets about their purchase. There are many steps to take when it comes to investing in a property. Ensure that you are going through the steps and taking your time to ensure you are making the right investment for you and your needs.

Make Sure You're Ready

The first rule of buying a property is to make sure that you are actually ready to do so. This means being financially and emotionally ready because buying a property is a huge commitment. You will also need to consider whether buying a property right now will fit into your goals for the future. Consider how buying this property is going to affect your finances and your life for the foreseeable future. You may even want to list out a few pros and cons to get a balanced idea of where you are when making this huge investment.

Get Your Finances in Order

As you already know, purchasing a property is a huge financial commitment. In fact, it is one of the biggest financial decisions you can make. You'll have to take some time to look at your finances to see whether you can afford a property right now. Have a look at your current finances, including your income, debts, assets, and liabilities. Consider whether you could afford a down payment on the property and the subsequent monthly mortgage payments.

After you have looked at your finances, you may conclude that you cannot afford a property right now. That's completely fine, and it's much better to be honest with yourself from the beginning. The next step from here is planning your finances so that you will be able to purchase a property in the future. This may mean cutting down on your expenses so that you can save toward a down payment. It may also mean that you should be looking for ways to increase your income so that managing the mortgage payments will be easier for you. Understanding your finances will help you plan for your future real estate investments.

The Down Payment

Once you know how much you can afford or whether you can afford a property at all, it is time to save for your down payment. It is advisable to save about 20 percent of the price of the property as a down payment. The reason is that a larger down payment will decrease your monthly mortgage payment and make it easier for you to pay off the mortgage quickly.

With that being said, you do not need to put down 20 percent. Many people choose to put down a smaller down payment and then increase their monthly mortgage payments in order to pay off the mortgage quickly. Whatever you decide, it is important to have some money saved for your down payment before you start aggressively looking for properties. Once you have the down payment, the purchasing process is going to happen a lot more quickly because you can put in an offer and then make the payments almost immediately. If you are looking for property now and don't have the money for a down payment, it may mean that all of this is wasted effort because you cannot put in an offer or get a mortgage.

Find the Right Mortgage

Many types of mortgages and home loans are offered by a variety of financial service providers. When you are looking for a mortgage, you must take the time to compare quotes from as many financial service providers as possible. You should also look at the different types of mortgages to see which one suits your needs the best. Applying for the right type of mortgage will significantly increase your chances of getting the mortgage and make the entire process easier for you.

Start Preapprovals

Once you have decided which mortgage and which mortgage lender you want to go for, you can start the preapproval process. Apply for mortgages with various lenders at the same time. This is an excellent strategy because even if you get denied by one lender, you still have others who could approve your mortgage. Just make sure that you are happy with all the financial service providers and types of mortgages you are applying for. You will need to gather financial paperwork and fill out multiple forms to start the preapproval process. However, it is a lot easier to do everything in bulk because once you have sent the documents to one lender, you can simply use the same financial documents for all the others.

Get a Real Estate Agent

Having a real estate agent on board is going to make the entire process of looking for the right property much easier. You can look on your own, but you will not have access to all the connections and options that a real estate agent does. On top of that, real estate agents can be a really important asset when it's your first time investing in a property, as they can guide you through things that you may not have thought of.

You don't have to go with the first agent you meet with. You can interview a few real estate agents and see which one suits your needs the best. Asking your friends and family members which real estate agents they have used is a great way to figure out which agents are reputable and professional. You always want an agent who will be on your side and will help negotiate on your behalf.

Go Shopping

Now starts the fun part of the process. You get to look for your property. Your real estate agent will guide you to different sites and send you properties that match your needs and budget. Have a look at a variety of property listing websites and just start scrolling through until you find properties that suit your needs. Once you have decided on a few different properties, you can actually visit and do walk-throughs of your ideal properties. When you visit the properties, take some photos and write a list of pros and cons so that you can keep track of which properties you like the most and why. If the market is hot and there are many people looking for real estate in that area, you may not have a lot of time to make your decision. This is why it is important to keep track of your thoughts so that you know exactly whether this property is for you if you need to put in an offer quickly.

Make an Offer

Once you have found the property of your dreams, it is time to make an offer. This is when you tell the current owner of the property that you want to make a purchase and then let them know how much you're willing to pay. You can go back to your real estate agent and ask how much they are expecting and how much you should be offering. Once you put in the offer, it is the seller's turn to accept or reject it. If they reject the offer, you have the opportunity to make a counteroffer that might be more appealing to them. This may start discussions between you and them until you can find an offer that both parties are happy with. Sometimes, the seller will not accept your offer; in that case, you have to move on and find another property to invest in.

Get a Mortgage

If the offer is accepted, then you move on to getting a mortgage. At this stage, you should already have preapprovals, so you can choose a lender who has preapproved you. This process involves a lot of paperwork, so it is a good idea to ask your real estate agent what is required in your area for a mortgage. This way, you can get everything collected, so when you apply for the mortgage, it is a much easier process. Some documents that you need are your W-2 forms, pay slips for the last two months, proof of income, tax certificates, bank statements, details on any loans, and your personal details, such as your ID and Social Security number.

Get Homeowner's Insurance

In some cases, mortgage lenders will not give you a loan unless you have homeowner's insurance. Even if the mortgage lender does not state this is a requirement, getting homeowner's insurance is a good idea to protect you and your investment. The policy should only become effective on the closing date or the date of sale. The insurer will help you along in this process.

Home Inspection

Before the deal is closed, it is important to do a home inspection to make sure you know exactly what you're getting into. Even if you have visited the property, you could have missed underlying problems that could end up costing you a lot of money once the house is in your possession. Getting a professional to do the home inspection is the best way to go. If you find anything that was not disclosed in the initial stage, then you can bring it to the seller's attention, and you might be able to negotiate a lower price, or you might decide that you no longer want to purchase the property. Regardless of the outcome, it is definitely better to know what you're getting into before you proceed with the purchase.

Have the Home Appraised

Home appraisal is different from the inspection that was done in the previous step. When you get your home appraised, you are figuring out how much it is worth. Typically, your mortgage lender will organize the appraisal even though you will be paying for it. The lender will need to know exactly how much the house is worth before they give you the mortgage.

Negotiate Any Repairs

You are now nearing the end of the process, so it is time to negotiate. This can be done face-to-face or through your real estate agents. If there are any repairs needed, you can start negotiating these with the property seller. Remember to be realistic, as the outcome of the negotiations will depend on the kind of market you are currently in.

Close the Deal

Once you're happy with everything, it is time to close the deal. This means that you and the seller have now agreed on the terms of the sale, and your mortgage has been approved. Some closing documents will need to be filled out. At this stage, you will probably be asked to do a final walk-through of the property. This is to make sure everything is as it should be. Once all that is done, you can close the deal, and you are now a property owner.

QUESTIONS TO ASK BEFORE BUYING

You are going to be putting down a lot of money when you purchase your property, so it is important that you ask the right questions. You are free to ask any questions you would like when negotiating or deciding whether you want to purchase a property. It is far better to ask more questions than fewer questions. Here are a few that you should consider before you make an offer or make a purchase:

- How old is the house?
- When were the major appliances installed?
- How long until these appliances need maintenance or replacement?

- Were any major renovations done, and if so, when?
- Do you have any paperwork on the house's repairs, appliances, and systems?
- Are there any water-related or electrical issues with the house?
- Has the property been bought or sold multiple times? If so, what were the reasons for this?
- Are there any negative aspects or history with this property?
- Is there anything else that I would need to know?

THE UNDERWRITING PROCESS

Underwriting is a very important part of the process when it comes to purchasing a property. This is not done by you but by the financial service provider. The process involves evaluating and assessing any financial and risk-related aspects of the investment. Essentially, the financial service provider is doing the due diligence to determine whether or not it is feasible to invest or lend you money. If you are a professional real estate investor, then you will probably have some underwriters on your team who do this for you to make sure the investments are viable and good options for your goals.

When the underwriting process is underway, a few different things are done. One of the first things is a financial analysis, in which all the financial aspects of the investment are looked into. This will include the potential for income, expenses, cash flow, and other financial aspects that need analysis. At the end of the day, when you are a property investor, you want to make sure that your property is going to bring in an income.

Risk assessment and cash flow analysis are also done during this process to make sure that no unnecessary risk is being taken and that the property will be in a good position to have a positive cash flow. Market analysis will also need to be done to consider the effect the current real estate market may have on the income potential and the general viability of a property investment. Finally, the underwriting process needs to do its due diligence to gather and verify relevant information regarding the property. This is just to ensure all the information and reports are accurate so that potential issues are dealt with as soon as possible.

As a real estate investor, you can use techniques from under-writing in order to analyze and evaluate your potential real estate investment deals. The basics of underwriting are to assess risk and ensure that your investments will be viable in the future. You can conduct your own underwriting analysis since you will have access to the majority of the data and information needed. You can also get a third party involved to assist you with the underwriting process. This can be done by a financial advisor or a broker who will identify any blind spots or issues that you may have missed when you did your own financial and risk analysis. The under-writing process is important because it allows you to plan your future and mitigate risk when investing in property. Investing in property is definitely exciting, but it is important not to get carried away with the process. If there are any red flags, you should defi-nitely take a step back and think about whether it is worth it. Property investors will tell you that there are deals that you simply have to walk away from after you have done the necessary analy-sis. It is far better to walk out on a potentially risky deal than be stuck in a situation where you are hemorrhaging money unnec-essarily.

Underwriting is part of the process in which you prepare to buy a property. Many of the steps we discussed in the first section of this chapter apply to underwriting. For example, you will need to gather all of your information and documentation, fill out the necessary forms, be responsive and available to your underwriters throughout the process, and ensure that any financial activities you participate in are relevant to purchasing this property. When you're going through the process of purchasing a property, it is important to be very cautious about what you are doing in the financial space, as opening any new lines of credit or taking out a loan could be a complication in the assessment that will be done. You don't want anything to impede the underwriting process or the property purchasing process.

DUE DILIGENCE

This is the time between your offer for the property being accepted and the closing of the deal. At this stage, it is important to ensure you review all the aspects of the deal and the transaction before you close. This stage is put in place to ensure that you are happy with the deal and that there are no red flags that you might have missed through the other steps of the process. If you find something that doesn't sit well with you, or there has been miscommunication or outright deception regarding the property, then you are free to cancel the deal. Just because the offer has been accepted does not mean that it has been finalized.

After the offer has been made, the true process of due diligence really starts. The first thing that happens is a home inspection. This is a more formal home visit than the one that you might've done before you made the offer. You will get a property inspector to come in and identify any issues with the property. If any major issues have been found, then you can back out, or you can negotiate with the seller of the property to bring the price down or have them resolve the issues before you move in.

Next comes a home appraisal, which will evaluate the property's market value based on various factors. Once this is done, a title check will need to be conducted. This is done to ensure there aren't any lawsuits or claims on the property that either you or the current owner are not aware of or have not disclosed. This is done to protect you from any potential legal expenses you may not be prepared for down the road. The next step in the process is a land or property survey. This is done in order to map out and locate features, boundaries, improvements, and corners of the land your property is on. The goal of this survey is to show you exactly where your property ends and another property begins. In many areas, this survey may already exist and can be passed on from seller to buyer.

Enlisting the service of a real estate attorney is necessary to review all contracts and legal documents related to the purchase. This is a complicated process, and you don't want to miss something or make a mistake that could cost you down the line. The lawyer takes care of things like examining the purchase agreement, disclosure statements, and any documents from the homeowners association (HOA) or zoning regulations. A real estate attorney is someone on your side to give you valuable insight into potential legal issues and ensure that your interests are always protected.

Another important part of the process is disclosures, in which the seller needs to disclose all information about the property in a written document. What they disclose will depend on the laws in the local area and those on a federal and state level. You can talk with your real estate agent or legal advisor about what exactly the seller needs to disclose to you. Certain things will always need to be disclosed, regardless of where you live, including any health and safety risks and the presence of potentially dangerous substances like asbestos and lead paint.

Every area will have its own rules, dependent on the neighborhood or area. This is where a homeowners association comes in. Not all properties are covered by a homeowners association, but if the one you are considering is, you'll need to know what they expect and any bylaws or covenants that you will be bound to if you decide to purchase that property. Some HOAs have restrictions on renting out your property, decorations, and even design choices, such as the color of your house paint. There are also fees attached to HOAs, which must be disclosed to you as soon as possible. The fees cover any public areas and protection that the HOA might take care of.

Next comes the zoning rules, which will show you what the property is allowed to be used for within the community. For example, if you are purchasing a property in a place where local flora and fauna are abundant, laws and rules may prevent you from building and encroaching on this flora and fauna. These zoning rules might be a deterrent for you to continue with the purchase of the property, so it is important to understand this aspect to make sure you know what you are allowed to do and what you are restricted from.

Finally, you will also have to consider insurance, as many mortgage brokers do not lend money to those who do not have homeowner's insurance. There is no law that suggests you should purchase homeowner's insurance, but it will impact your eligibility to get a mortgage or home loan. Homeowner's insurance is also important to protect you and your home. If anything major were to happen to your property, it would come at a hefty price, so having this insurance would cover these planned situations. The type of homeowner's insurance that you need will depend on the property location and risk factors. For example, if you live in an area where floods are common, then you would need flood insurance tacked on to your insurance policy. Speaking to an insurance broker is the best way to go about this process.

ESTIMATING COSTS FOR RENOVATION DURING PROPERTY ANALYSIS

During the property analysis process, certain areas of maintenance may arise that you will need to address. Your property assessor will look through all the different aspects of the property and then assess whether repairs or renovations are needed. In case you take on repairs, it is important to understand the common renovations when purchasing a property. This could help you mentally prepare should you need to do them. Some of these renovations include roofing, plumbing, electrical work, drywall, pest removal, garbage disposals, and HVAC (Heating, Ventilation, and Air Conditioning) systems.

It can be difficult to estimate the cost of renovations and improvements, but having a roundabout number to work with is important. This is going to help you budget effectively so you can ensure you are renovating properly and have the finances to do so. On top of that, estimating the renovation cost can also help you negotiate with the seller. If there are renovations that are going to cost you a lot and you're willing to do them, then you can negotiate down the price.

Many factors come into play when talking about renovations. The price of a renovation depends on various factors, including the scope of the project, the labor and materials needed, and the duration of the work. You will also need to consider the cost based on your area or region, as labor and supplies vary depending on where you are. The range for any kind of repair or renovation is incredibly wide, so it's not helpful to guess if you do not have specific numbers or know precisely what the renovations are going to entail.

When trying to estimate any kind of renovation, the first thing you need to do is know what renovations will have to be done. You can start researching labor and materials needed for the renovation. It is a good idea to start calling around and contacting the relevant professionals who will be taking care of the renovations. They will send you a quote based on the information you give them, and then you can start comparing quotes. If you have done a home inspection, then you should have a good idea of what needs to be done on the property and can then give this information to the relevant professionals. If you are doing these renovations as an add-on or addition to your property, then you will need to let the professionals who will be doing the renovations know exactly what you are planning to do.

The first person you should get in contact with is a general contractor, as they will be taking care of a majority of the processes. These are the people who have contacts with other relevant professionals in the industry. It may be difficult for you to know who to get into contact with if you do not know what is needed. The general contractor will come in and have a look at your vision and needs, and then both of you can work on a plan going forward and bring in other contractors, such as plumbers and electricians. You are under no obligation to go with the first quote you get, and it is definitely important to shop around so you can find the best deals for your renovations.

INTERACTIVE ELEMENT: DUE DILIGENCE CHECKLIST

Due diligence is an extremely important step when it comes to purchasing a property. You want to ensure you are doing your research to avoid any problems down the line. Here is a checklist you can use for this process.

Pre-offer

- Population growth
- Income levels of households in the area
- Vacancies in the area
- Average and median rent prices
- School ratings
- Property value
- Crime rates

Financial Due Diligence

- Potential gross rental income
- Any other income you could make from the property
- Expenses
- Cost of maintenance and repairs
- Taxes
- Insurance
- Contributions to an emergency savings account for property issues and improvements

Post-offer

- Home inspection by a professional
- Utilities and mechanical systems
- Overall condition of all rooms
- Outside areas, such as the driveway and garden
- Mold and termite inspection
- Flood zone verification

Financial Due Diligence

- Profit/loss statements for two years prior
- Previous owner's income tax return
- Current rent
- Lease terms
- Additional fees charged to renters
- List of repairs and capital improvements
- Existing service contracts
- Taxes

With the property purchase process and renovation planning covered, it's essential to understand the tax benefits and legal considerations of real estate investing. We now go into the third part of the framework.

TELL YOUR STORY TO INSPIRE OTHERS

"If you want to go somewhere, it is best to find someone who has already been there."

— ROBERT KIYOSAKI

The further you get into your journey with real estate investment, the more questions people will have for you. How did you do it? Is it really something that anyone can do? You'll be able to tell them your story and encourage them as they start considering whether they, too, could get started with real estate investment—but unless you decide to dedicate your life to guiding others through the process, you're probably not going to have the time to walk them through every little thing they need to do.

Guiding people through the process has become something of a passion of mine, and it's this that led me to write about both real estate investment and setting up an Airbnb business. I want to make this process as easy and accessible as possible for those with big dreams but little experience, and I want people to realize that this is a much more realistic option than they might have imagined. Essentially, I want to answer all the questions that you're probably going to be asked as you start seeing success with real estate investment... and that means you have a very easy way to help people who are inspired by your journey—all you have to do is point them in the direction of this book!

I'd also like to encourage you to share this book on a wider scale so that I can help more people through this process. All you need to do to make a big difference is leave a short review online.

By leaving a review of this book on Amazon, you'll show new readers exactly where they can find all the information they need to get started with real estate investment—and find a solid route to success.

Reviews are so helpful in connecting books with their intended audiences, and simply by leaving your feedback, you can help others find the information they're looking for quickly. This, combined with any friends or family members you pass this on, will make a huge difference to anyone interested in exploring real estate investment.

Thank you so much for your support. I truly appreciate it.

Scan the QR code below

PART III

PROFIT AND PROSPER

6

TAX BENEFITS AND LEGAL CONSIDERATIONS

W hen Brendon started his real estate investment journey, something that nobody told him about was the tax benefits. In his first year of running a short-term rental, he brought an accountant on board to help him with the general finances and his taxes since his financial situation had changed. He sat with the accountant, who explained to him the various tax deductions and benefits he could take advantage of through his investments. He was quite surprised as he worked through the list of tax-deductible expenses and items. He never knew that owning an investment property not only increased his income but also reduced his taxable income. This was a big win for him because, like most of us, he's not a big fan of paying unnecessary taxes.

TAX BENEFITS

Real estate investments can help you reduce your taxable income, which is one of the major benefits of investing in real estate. It is important to understand these tax benefits because you don't want to pay more tax than is necessary. Reducing your taxable income means that you have additional finances to put into other areas of your life and even back into your investments. You can speak to a professional accountant or tax advisor for some specific advice, but there are some key areas to be aware of when you are a real estate investor.

One of the most obvious tax benefits of real estate investing is the write-offs that you get with it. A write-off means that you're not taxed on the amount you spend in these areas, which lowers your overall taxable income and results in paying fewer taxes. These tax write-offs include property taxes, insurance, interest on your mortgage, property management fees, and any costs you have to repair or maintain your property. Those are the most common write-offs, but you can also get them if you run your real estate investment as a business since there are business expenses that can be tax write-offs, too. These include business equipment, travel, advertising, fees for legal services, and accounting.

Another tax benefit is depreciation, which is the loss of your property's value over time. If your property produces income, such as a rental property, you will be able to deduct depreciation as an expense and lower your taxable income. You will also have tax benefits through capital gains, which is the amount you will make if you sell your property. This can be divided into short-term and long-term capital gains. Short-term capital gains occur when you buy and sell a property within a year. Long-term capital gains are if you are in possession of the property for more than a year, and capital gains in this category have a much lower tax rate, which is more beneficial to you.

Another wonderful tax benefit that comes with real estate is that if you have rental property and are earning income, you effectively avoid the FICA tax. This payroll tax applies to self-employed individuals who earn an income. If you are self-employed and earn an income through most other avenues, the money you earn is taxed on payroll tax since this person will need to pay for both the employer and the employee portion of the FICA tax. However, if your rental property is considered passive income (as are most long-term rentals), it is not liable for this kind of tax, so you avoid it completely.

1031 EXCHANGE

A tax benefit that needs its own section in this chapter is called the 1031 exchange. This is a strategy in which you defer taxes when you take the profit gained from selling one property and invest in another property. When you take the money out of an investment, you are liable for capital gains tax, but with the 1031 exchange option, you can skip capital gains tax by investing the money from the old property into a new investment property. This is a great way for investors to lower their taxes or at least defer for a significant amount of time.

A process needs to be followed if you want to go this route. The first thing you will need to do is figure out which property you want to sell and which you are going to buy. You have to have properties in mind in order to make the exchange. On top of that, the properties you wish to make this exchange between need to be very similar, even if they're not the same quality and one is more expensive or has a higher value than the other. For example, you would not be able to use the 1031 exchange if you own a one-bedroom apartment and want to exchange it for a vacation home.

This is not the kind of thing that can be done on your own, so you will need an intermediary. This person acts as an exchange facilitator and will handle the transaction. The person or company needs to be qualified, and they will hold your sale in escrow until the exchange has been completed. They will handle most of the process, including coordinating with the seller of the property so they fully understand the implications of the exchange and the process going forward. They will also prepare all the documentation for you and the seller of the new property to make sure the exchange happens successfully and smoothly. The funds from the sale will remain in escrow until the sale is complete, which means the money will be out of your account and be held separately. If everything is successful, the money will be transferred to the seller, but if things don't go according to plan, you will get your money back. They will also guide you through all the paperwork, including the change of title on the deed and property.

There are many requirements for the 1031 exchange, and it is important to understand them before you go through with this process. Firstly, the properties being exchanged need to be of a like kind. You need to ensure that the properties are similar in nature and function for the exchange to occur. Another important consideration is that you will not have access to the proceeds from the sale of your property. If you take any proceeds from the sale, that will be taxable income, and you would not have taken full advantage of the 1031 exchange.

There are timeline requirements that need to be followed in order for this exchange to be successful. First off is the forty-five-day rule. This rule states that you have forty-five days after you sell your property to find a replacement property. You will need to identify this property in writing and include a description of the new property. Then there is the 180-day rule, which specifies you have to close the sale of the replacement property within 180 days of selling your relinquished property. If you do not meet this deadline, you will need to pay capital gains tax on the profit you made from the sale of the initial property you had in your position. Since these timelines are quite short, it may be a good idea to find the exchange property well in advance and start the conversation with the seller of the property. This way, things may go a lot more smoothly, and you will not be at risk of not meeting the deadlines for the 1031 exchange.

LEGAL CONSIDERATIONS

The legal aspects of investing in property are so important. While it might be tempting to skip legal considerations and just throw your money at investments, this is definitely not the most beneficial way to invest in real estate. There are many legal considerations that you will have to contemplate. Knowing what these are is going to help you put your best foot forward.

The first thing you want to do is understand the local regulations where you want to invest. Every city, country, and area is governed by different regulations. This means that what may be legal in one area is completely illegal in another. The local regulations dictate many things, including the type of property development, rental regulations, and zoning laws. Before you even consider investing in a property, ensure you fully understand all local regulations. You can easily find this on the municipality or state's website. If you are concerned about something, then it is worth getting a property lawyer involved to help explain things to ensure you have all the knowledge you need. You definitely don't want to be in the process of making a real estate investment only to realize that you cannot use it in the way you wanted due to overlooked legal considerations.

As you know from Chapter 5, doing your due diligence is essential when it comes to investing in real estate. Legal due diligence has many aspects, but they are all important. The first thing you will need to do is do a title search to make sure that the title is free and that you will be able to take ownership rights of that property. You also need to do a property inspection and survey the property to make sure that you are not being given false information. You want to ensure that you get exactly what you think you'll be getting when you purchase that property. Another part of due diligence is environmental considerations, such as hazards or contaminations. You may need to get a professional involved to evaluate any potential environmental risks currently on the property or that could arise based on what you want to do with your property once you've purchased it.

When you are ready to start negotiating and creating a contract, doing your due diligence in this area is important, too. You definitely don't want to be signing any documents without making sure that you are protected. There will be a lot of paperwork in the process of purchasing a property, and you don't want to overlook any important areas. You can get a real estate lawyer involved to help review contracts and negotiate favorable terms so you are not missing out. There may be potential risks in the contract negotiation that you could miss simply because you do not have all the knowledge. If you choose to go through the process yourself, make sure that you are doing the relevant research and reading through the contract meticulously. If you find a clause or statement that raises a red flag, ensure that you do your research about it and reach out if you need help. It is better to sort this out well in advance rather than being stuck in a contract that is unfavorable to you and your investments.

If your goal is to rent out your property and become a landlord, then it is essential that you understand tenant and landlord laws in the area in which you are investing. You must understand the world and responsibilities of a landlord before you take on that obligation. Being a landlord is not simply renting out your property and then never seeing it again. You have to take care of the maintenance, rental agreement, payments, structure, eviction processes, and any tenancy issues. It is a lot of responsibility, so it is important to understand what you are responsible for and what the tenant's part will be. Knowing this before you become a land-lord is important so you can prepare yourself and decide whether you want to do this.

The legal aspects of owning and using a property as an investment are important. You must take the time to understand all legal aspects and do your due diligence in all areas. While this can take some time and effort, you will definitely be thankful that you went through the process. It will save you a lot of time, money, effort, and heartache in the future if you put in the effort now.

Now that we've covered tax benefits and legal considerations, let's discuss generating passive income through rental properties.

PASSIVE INCOME THROUGH LONG-TERM RENTALS

When you're using your real estate investment as passive income, long-term rentals tend to be one of the best options. There are many reasons for this, including the fact that you are making a rental income and earning money through capital growth, getting tax benefits, and diversifying your assets. Taking the time to understand this type of investment strategy is really going to help you see whether it is a good fit for you. Plus, you get to explore the world of rentals and understand the topic at a deeper level.

LONG-TERM RENTALS

A long-term rental is a rental property that you lease out to a tenant for a longer period. These leases can vary in length, but they fall under the umbrella of long-term rental if you are renting out your property to somebody for more than six months.

Benefits

There are many benefits to investing in long-term rentals. Many real estate investors choose to do this due to the benefits and stability it offers. In this section, we are going to talk about the many benefits that come from long-term rentals.

Monthly Rental Income

One of the most obvious benefits is the fact that you are getting a monthly rental income. Since you are renting out the property on a long-term basis, it means that you're making a passive income by getting rental income every month. This stable form of income is predictable and comes in at an agreed-upon date. It allows you to budget and plan, and you know that you are going to get your money.

Depreciation/Tax Deductions

When you own a long-term rental, you have some tax advantages, including writing off certain expenses. For example, you'll be able to write off the interest on your mortgage and depreciation of your assets on your tax forms. This effectively lowers your taxable income, and you will be paying less tax.

Building Equity

If you have a mortgage on your rental property, then you can use your rental income to put toward your mortgage and build equity into your investment. This means that you are paying down the amount you owe so that you own more of the property yourself. You can leverage this equity into other investments or leave it as is, so even if you do have to sell your property before you pay off the entire mortgage, the amount of money you can take out of the property will be a lot more.

Property Appreciation

When a property appreciates in value, it means it is increasing in value over time. Now, there is no guarantee that your property will appreciate in value; however, if you have made a good investment, it is highly likely that your property will increase in value. When you have a rental property, you are making an income from two different areas. The first one is your rental income, and then you're also making money through the property's appreciation in value. While property appreciation might not feel like it is bringing in an income at the moment, when it comes time to sell the property, you will get a lot more than what you purchased it for. You can sell your property for profit when you need to.

Leverage on Investment

If there comes a time when you want to start investing in more than one property or in different kinds of properties, then it is good to know that you can leverage your current properties to do so. You can get a mortgage or loan on a second property by leveraging your first property so that you can get more investments and increase your investment income exponentially. This needs to be done very carefully, as there is a risk when you leverage one property in order to buy more properties. However, if you can make the right investment choices and do your research, you will definitely put yourself in a position for success.

Tips and Tricks

Investing in real estate and rental properties has a learning curve. As you become a more experienced investor, you will learn the nuances that come with this type of investment. With that being said, you want to set yourself up for success from the beginning, so following a few tips and tricks may help you do just that.

Choose the Right Neighborhoods

The neighborhood of the property you want to invest in is going to be crucial for making the most profit. Before you even consider investing in a property, you should do some research on the neighborhood. Even a simple drive through the neighborhood can tell you a lot. An area that is safe and close to good schools, amenities, transportation, shopping centers, and recreational activities is going to be the best neighborhood to invest in.

People always want to live in areas like that, so there will be a demand. When there is a demand for property in an area, a real estate investor can make more money. You will find it a lot easier to find tenants who want to stay in the neighborhood for a long time. When your goal is to make a passive income, getting people who want to live in the neighborhood for an extended period is going to be incredibly beneficial. Many people are willing to rent for five, ten, or even twenty years if they like the neighborhood and want to put down roots there. In this case, you now have a passive stream of income for many years, and you don't have to go through the process of finding new tenants or taking care of a property. Most of the work is done for you, and you can just generate an income.

Locate Profitable Investments

The type of property that you invest in is almost as important as the neighborhood. The property type needs to make sense for the tenant you want to welcome into the home. Properties with more bedrooms and bathrooms will attract bigger families who typically have children. However, smaller properties may attract people who are single or who are just starting out in their lives. This means the amount of money you can charge for rent is going to change. On top of that, how you go about finding your tenants and managing the property is going to differ depending on the type of property you have.

For example, a luxury property will be a little more difficult to market and find tenants for. That is because there is less of a market for luxury properties. However, a single-family home is more appealing to the public, which means it will be a lot easier for you to find tenants. For a beginner investor, a single-family home tends to be the best option. This can be a standalone house, townhouse, or even an apartment.

Look at the Numbers

It is all good to find a beautiful property that you want to invest in, but it is essential that you look at the numbers before you make any kind of investment. The numbers are going to tell you whether the property is going to make a successful investment or if it's going to be a liability. If you have a few properties in mind for your investment, then you can compare the numbers to see which one is going to be the most beneficial investment.

In order to compare the numbers for the different properties, you will need to look at the expenses, cash flow, and potential income from those properties. This is great to assist you in making the best decisions regarding your property investments and ensure that you are not choosing something that will look good on the outside but won't bring in the returns you want.

PRICING STRATEGY

Your pricing strategy is an incredibly important part of your rental investment. If you price your rent too low, it means that you are leaving money on the table, and you might not be making enough to cover your costs. You don't put yourself in a position where you are essentially losing money when making a profit is possible. If you overprice your property, you may end up struggling to find people to rent the space, which will also end up costing you money since you will have vacancies. The goal is to find the sweet spot when it comes to pricing, where you can maximize your profits and ensure you can afford all your expenses.

Know Your Competition

You may have a number in mind that you think you deserve for your rental property, but it is important to know your competition and situate competitively. There is probably a range in which people in the area are willing to pay for property similar to yours. If you set your rent too high, you will put yourself in a position where it is difficult to find tenants. If you set your rent too low, it means that you'll either attract bad tenants or you will be losing money.

Knowing what is going on in your neighborhood will help you set a competitive rate for your rent to maximize your profit and ensure that you have people interested in renting your property. You can go onto property websites to see how much people are charging for rent on properties similar to yours. When doing this research, ensure that you are looking for properties with features and amenities similar to your property. That is what's going to give you the most accurate idea of how much people will pay.

Property prices tend to shift over time, so make sure you check at least every few weeks. This way, you can shift your rental rates to keep your property relevant and competitive in the market.

The 2 Percent Rule Is Just a Guideline

One rule that many landlords tend to stick to is the 2 percent rule. This rule states that you should be charging up to 2 percent of your property's value as rent each month. It makes it easy for you to set a price for monthly rent. This is definitely just a guideline and shouldn't be something that you follow strictly. There is so much to consider when it comes to setting rental prices that it's simply not beneficial for you to stick to this rule without doing any additional research.

Seasonality Matters

You may think that the weather has nothing to do with whether people are looking to rent a property or not, but that is not true. Depending on where you live, there may be differences in seasonality, but the general trend seems to be that people are more likely to move—and look for new properties to live in—during the warmer months. This is probably because it is easier to move when it is warmer. However, in very hot climates, extreme heat can also deter people from relocating. People are generally more willing to stay put in the colder months when they just want to stay indoors. This is especially so if you live in a very cold climate, as it can be incredibly inconvenient and unappealing to move houses in a snowstorm or when children are in the full swing of the school year.

Since the demand for property tends to be lower in the colder months, you may need to price your rent much lower in order to attract potential tenants. If you are going for a long-term rental strategy, this could have a huge negative financial impact on your overall income. If at all possible, you should spend most of your time marketing your property in the summer months so you can get your renters moved in and settled, so you do not have to worry about it in the winter months.

Consider Your Property's Amenities

The price you set for your rental property will not just be based on the property itself. The number of bedrooms and bathrooms is incredibly important, but there are other things that people look for. That is why it is important to consider your amenities, both on the property and in the surrounding area. There are many amenities that people look for and will pay a little extra for. One of these is safe parking. This could be in the form of a garage, assigned parking, or safe street parking. People do not want to park far away and have to walk down the street in order to get home. This means they will be willing to pay a little bit extra if there is safe parking on or close to the property, or if the property is conveniently located near public transit.

Another key aspect is the general safety of the property and the area. If there is some sort of added security, this will give your tenants peace of mind. This kind of security could be a gated community or even smart home technology and security systems installed in the home. People also look at the safety of the general area and whether it is walkable or not. Walkability means that the property is going to be close to local shops and services and that it's safe to walk on the streets.

Another highly beneficial feature that can increase a property's price is outdoor features and entertainment areas. A pool, patio, balcony, or any kind of recreational area is hugely beneficial. This doesn't have to be directly on the property. For example, if there is a tennis court or communal pool nearby or shared by the same cluster of properties, then this will increase your potential rent prices.

TENANT SCREENING

Once you have set up your pricing strategy and are ready to welcome new tenants, it is time to consider the tenant screening process. One of the biggest mistakes that first-time investors make is allowing anyone to rent their property just so they can get an income. Your tenants can make your life much easier or create huge difficulties for you. This is why it is so important to have a robust tenant screening process to ensure you are choosing the right tenants. You want to make sure that the people who live on your property are going to pay on time, take care of your property, and be responsible.

When you put out advertisements for your rental property, you are probably going to get some interest. You should take some time to research all your potential tenants, even though it may be a little more trouble. Certain things are essential to ask your potential tenants about so you can get some data on them to see whether they would be a good fit. With regard to paying their rent on time and being able to afford the rent, you will need their proof of income and creditworthiness. A good rule of thumb is to look for tenants who make more than three times the monthly rent you will be charging. This safe zone shows that your potential tenants can afford to live on the property. It is a good idea to ask for a three- to six-month bank statement to make sure that they have been earning a steady income. In order to check their creditworthiness, you will need to have a look at their credit history and their credit score. If they are good at managing their credit, it means that they are less likely to fall behind with their rent payments and have proven that they managed their finances well.

Next, you will need to check whether they are good people who live responsible lives. You can check their criminal background, eviction history, and their references. You definitely don't want somebody to live on your property who will put the neighbors in danger, so make sure you run a background check to ensure that the potential tenant did not participate in activities that could put your property or people living in the surrounding area at risk. Checking eviction history helps you to see whether this person is a good tenant. Always find out why the tenant was evicted. If it was because of a violation of the lease agreement or any kind of illegal conduct, damages, or missing rent payments, then you know this person may not be a good fit for you. Finally, you will need to have a look at their references, as these will give you a good indication of their character and whether they have been good tenants in the past. It is definitely a red flag if their references don't have anything particularly good to say about them. After the screening process, you will have a much better idea of whether this person is a good fit for you.

SELF-MANAGEMENT VERSUS PROPERTY MANAGEMENT

For managing your rental property, you have two choices. You can either choose to manage it yourself or get a property manager on board to do it for you. Let's start talking about the self-management method and the pros and cons that come with it.

PROS AND CONS OF SELF-MANAGEMENT

Pros

Saving on Fees

Property management comes at a fee, so if you are doing it yourself, you are saving money. You don't have to pay yourself to take care of the property, so you can put this money into other areas of your investment or simply save it for yourself.

Doing Things Yourself

There is something to be said for doing things yourself. You're able to do things your way, and there is no risk of misunderstandings or miscommunications with somebody else. If you enjoy taking on a challenge and doing things yourself, this could be a good route for you.

Choosing Tenants

Managing your property means that you get to be the one to choose the tenants. With a big investment like real estate, there is peace of mind when you make the decisions yourself and choose the tenants based on your own criteria. You can also build a relationship with your tenants that can lead to mutual respect.

Cons

Takes Commitment

Managing a property by yourself takes commitment and a lot of effort. It means you must be available should there be an emergency or if your tenants need you. Many smaller tasks that take up quite a bit of your time need to be taken care of consistently.

Legal Considerations

There are quite a few legalities when it comes to investing in real estate and renting out your property. A property manager will have all the necessary experience that a first-time investor may not have. It will take some extra work on your part to make sure that you understand all the legal processes and requirements so you don't end up in a sticky situation.

Requires Marketing

Doing things yourself also means you will have to market your property yourself. This can be challenging if you have never done it before. On top of that, many property managers have a network that can assist them with finding the right tenants for a property, and an individual investor may not have the same contacts.

Roles of a Property Manager

A property manager deals with many rules and responsibilities. This alleviates a lot of pressure from the investor. Understanding what a property manager does might help you decide whether this is somebody you want to bring onto your team.

Acquiring Tenants

A property manager will be responsible for acquiring the right tenant for the property. If a tenant's lease is up and they decide they no longer want to stay there, the property manager will start the process again and find a new tenant.

Collecting Rent and Handling Evictions

A property manager will also handle the strict tasks of collecting rent and handling any evictions that need to occur. If a tenant is not paying on time, the property manager will start the process of collecting that money and might need to get lawyers and other legal professionals on board. If this situation escalates, then the property manager will also need to handle evictions and all the necessary processes that follow.

Managing Tenant Requests

When you rent out your property, you become a landlord. This means that if anything were to go wrong on the property, the tenants could call you and request that you attend to the issues. If you have a property manager, your tenants will call them should they need anything or have any requests.

Taking Care of Accounting

Accounting is a very important part of managing a property and ensuring that it is running smoothly. Your property manager will take care of all the bookkeeping and make sure that you are making a profit and that money is going into the right areas.

PROS AND CONS OF PROPERTY MANAGEMENT

Now that you know what a property manager does, it is important to know the pros and cons. This will give you a broader understanding of property management so you can see both sides of the coin.

Pros

Easy and Stress-Free

Hiring a property manager means that the rental process is going to be a lot easier for you. You will not need to stress out about your tenant's maintenance of the property or any other aspect of being a landlord. You will only need to get involved if something very important requires your attention, and your property manager will contact you regarding this.

Understand the Market

Property managers will have experience in the real estate market, and that means they can make decisions with a wealth of knowledge. This might be something you do not have, so bringing this kind of professional on board could help you see better returns on your investment.

Build a Wall Between You and the Tenants

If you are the type of person who does not want to deal with the social aspects of having tenants, then a property manager is a great choice. It creates a barrier between you and your tenants, so you do not have to deal with them or have any direct contact with them.

Oversee Maintenance and Problems

Running a rental property means that maintenance needs to be taken care of and problems need to be solved. The property manager will call the tenant if there is a problem or if maintenance is needed in a certain area. The manager will also handle all maintenance schedules and ensure your property runs smoothly throughout the year.

Cons

Poor Performance

There is always a risk that your property manager will perform poorly and not meet your expectations. Therefore, it is essential to choose the right property manager, but sometimes, things go wrong, even with all the right steps being taken.

Troublesome Employees

When hiring a property manager, you are essentially relinquishing a lot of control to that person. This means they can hire staff or contractors to help with the maintenance, cleaning, and anything else on the property. There's always a risk of troublesome employees working on your property, and sometimes, this could even be the property managers themselves.

Loss of Revenues

When hiring a property manager, you have to pay them for their services. This is typically a percentage of your rent or revenue. The percentage will vary depending on the property manager or the company they work for. Often, this is somewhere between 5 and 10 percent.

Pay for Fees

On top of the percentage payment that you owe them, there may also be additional fees you need to pay. Some property management companies require a placement fee if they find a new tenant for your property. It is important to understand the contract when working with a property manager so you know what costs you might be liable for.

IDEAS TO GENERATE MORE INCOME FROM YOUR RENTAL PROPERTIES

You can make some additional income from your rental property in many ways. Some investors choose to stick to the basics and just generate revenue through the rent they charge, but you can get a little creative and expand your money-making opportunities. These ideas are not going to work for every property or for every investor.

However, you can try one or two of these options to increase the revenue you make through your rental properties.

Rent out fully furnished apartments and rooms. You can charge a bit more when you are renting out fully furnished apartments and rooms. People are more willing to spend when a living space is aesthetically decorated and taken care of.

Offer storage space. If you have additional space in your garage or spare room, you can offer it as a storage space. People are always looking for places to store their extra furniture and items.

Minimize resident turnover. If you are trying to ensure that your property makes the most profit, it is important to minimize your turnover. If you have long-term tenants, it means that you are getting a steady rental income without having to do much work. This means you must provide them with excellent service and ensure that you meet their needs.

Add services and amenities. See if you can add a service or amenity that could be beneficial to your tenants. For example, you could offer a laundry or cleaning service since this is something that people often need. You can add additional amenities like a pool, play area, or air conditioning to add greater benefits to your property.

Reinvest your profits. The money you make from your rental doesn't need to be spent immediately. Instead, you can use this money to reinvest to continue growing your profits. Even though you may not be using the money you're making immediately, you are increasing your overall net worth, and it will be valuable in the future.

Use dynamic pricing strategies. A dynamic pricing strategy means you change your prices based on what is going on in the market. If you are trying to find tenants when there is a lot of demand, then you can increase your prices since people will be willing to pay more. You can decrease your price and offer a discount to be more attractive and competitive in the quieter season.

Increase energy efficiency. Electricity and energy cost a lot of money, so get an energy professional into your property to see how you can use energy more efficiently. This can save you a lot of money in the long run, and it is also kinder to the environment.

INTERACTIVE ELEMENT: CREATING A PROPERTY MANAGEMENT PLAN

Creating a property management plan is crucial when it comes to running a rental property. Without a plan, things can get overlooked, and this will make things harder for you in the future. Follow these steps to create a robust property management plan.

Step 1: Taking Care of Your Property's Needs

Property's existing issues:

_____

_____

_____

Trends in the local rental market:

_____

_____

_____

Legal requirements:

_____

_____

_____

Step 2: Setting Goals

Long-term goals:

_____

_____

_____

Short-term goals:

_____

_____

_____

Financial goals:

_____

_____

_____

Tenant satisfaction goals:

_____

_____

_____

Property-specific goals:

_____

_____

_____

Step 3: Create Your Budget

Income:

Name	Amount

Expenses:

Name	Amount

Savings:

Name	Amount

Step 4: Make a Maintenance Schedule

Indoors:

Name	Budgeted Amount	Date

Outdoors:

Name	Budgeted Amount	Date

Plumbing:

Name	Budgeted Amount	Date

Electrical:

Name	Budgeted Amount	Date

Landscaping:

Name	Budgeted Amount	Date

HVAC:

Name	Budgeted Amount	Date

Other Upkeep:

Name	Budgeted Amount	Date

Now that you're familiar with long-term rentals, let's move on to short-term rentals and why they're profitable.

SHORT-TERM RENTALS

Active listings on Airbnb exceeded 7.7 million by the end of 2023, increasing 18 percent year-over-year with sustained double-digit supply growth across all regions. And in 2023 alone, hosts earned more than $57 billion (Airbnb, 2024). This shows how much money there is to be made through short-term rentals and platforms like Airbnb. If you have not considered short-term rentals, then this may be your sign to start thinking about it.

WHAT ARE SHORT-TERM RENTALS?

A short-term rental is also known as a vacation rental. It is a property the owner rents out to people who will only stay there for a short period. The property must be fully furnished, and all necessary amenities must be provided to the guests. With short-term rentals, we refer to the people staying in the property as guests rather than tenants because they are not staying there on a long-term basis. The guests are also not responsible for taking care of the property in the ways a tenant would. There are completely different expectations between the two, and the goal of a short-term rental business is to make sure there are consistent bookings of the property.

Short-term rental properties are a growing market. We are seeing it become more and more accessible through companies like Airbnb and VRBO. These are platforms where somebody with a property posts it as a listing, and people looking for a short-term rental can easily view and book. It is an alternative to a hotel so that guests can get a unique experience as well as competitive pricing. A host, or the owner of the property, also has a good chance to make even more money than with a long-term rental. This is because people are willing to pay more per night when they are booking a vacation or short-term stay. If you have good guest turnover, you will have a high chance of making good money through short-term rentals. As with anything, short-term rentals have pros and cons, and it's important to understand these before diving in.

PROS

Flexibility

There is a lot of flexibility in how you choose to run a short-term rental. If you only want to rent out your property on certain days, then you can do that. You can bring in guests as often or as seldom as you would like. Some people choose to rent their homes or their main property on a short-term rental basis when they are traveling. For example, if you plan a two-month European vacation, you can rent out your home to make additional money while you're not there. Another example of this flexibility would be if you have a rental property that is a bit farther away from you and you are only in the area on the weekends. You could choose to rent out your property on the weekends when you can attend to your guests, and it's most convenient for you.

Most of the short-term rental platforms and websites allow you to choose when you want to rent out your property. If there is a time when you do not want to accept guests, you can block that out on the calendar so people cannot book. This gives you complete control over when you are accepting guests and when it is going to be the most convenient for you.

Higher Cash Flow

With short-term rentals, you have the opportunity to make a lot of money. All you have to do is a bit of quick math to figure this out. A property could bring in $1,500 per month for rent on a long-term basis. Renting out a property as a vacation rental allows you to charge $1,500 for a week. That means you could potentially earn four times as much money using a short-term rental strategy.

The reason for this huge difference in pricing is that when you set a fee for a short-term rental, you are doing it on a per-night basis. But for a long-term rental, you have to set a per-month rental price that must be locked in for the duration of the lease. Something else to consider with short-term rentals is that you can change the nightly fee whenever you want. When vacation properties are in high demand, you can increase the price in order to generate more profit. You can also lower the price in the low-demand seasons to attract more people to your vacation rental. There are a lot of pricing strategies that you can use when it comes to short-term rentals that are simply not available with a long-term rental. This maximizes the amount of profit that you can make.

Fewer Tenant Legal Disputes

With a short-term rental, there is a lower likelihood of you having large legal disputes with your guests. A guest will typically stay for no longer than a week and then move on. However, with a long-term tenant, there are a lot of legal aspects to take into consideration. A prolonged tenant and landlord relationship can lead to legal action based on disagreements. These kinds of legal disputes can be costly as well as time-consuming.

It is important to note that there are tenant laws that protect short-term renters in the same way they might protect long-term rentals. Staying up-to-date with all the relevant property laws will make your life a lot easier in the long run. You will cover your back and ensure that you are meeting all the relevant legal standards.

CONS

Risk of Prolonged Vacancy

There are risks when it comes to short-term rentals. While the potential for a larger income is definitely there, there is also the risk of a prolonged vacancy. When this happens, you will not be making any money through rental income for the duration of the vacancy. There is no guarantee that you will get consistent bookings and guests. With a vacation rental, you have to understand the market. Some months are booming, and people are booking their vacations like crazy, while other months are much slower. In the slower months, you may struggle to get people to book with you, which means that you will be losing out.

With a prolonged vacancy, you will still be liable for the utilities on the property. With a long-term rental, the tenants have to pay the utilities, but this is not the case with a short-term rental. You will have to pay the mortgage and any other bills that come with the property, even if you're not making money at that moment. If there are prolonged vacancies, you will also need to make more of an effort to go and check on the property, as there is no one there to report potential issues like plumbing problems, damages, or electrical faults.

In seasons when there are not a lot of bookings, it is still important for you to maintain the general cleanliness of the property. You don't know when you will get new guests, and making a good impression is important. That means that even if nobody is in the property, you still have to make sure it is up to standard.

More Time and Property Upkeep

Since the guest turnover in a vacation rental property is high, you are required to spend more time on your rental property. This is not a passive income because you have to turn over the property and ensure it's ready for your next guest. When one guest checks out, you have to go in, clean the property, and make sure all the necessities have been replaced. Then, you will need to check in the new guests and make sure they have everything they need. You also have to be on call should your guests need something from you or have an emergency.

With short-term rentals, the goal is to give your guests the best experience possible. You will only get guests and have good ratings on the platform if you provide exceptional service. This means you will need to be there for your guests and provide them with the service they want.

You may also need to do regular maintenance and upkeep checks more often. Some guests may not be as careful as you would like them to be. Remember that when guests check into a place for a holiday, they don't want to think about anything serious. Their main goal is to relax or have fun. In that case, they might be a bit more careless with handling things, which means more maintenance is going to be required from you. Of course, they shouldn't destroy your property, but if they are a little clumsy with their luggage or decide to move around the furniture, then there will be scuffs and scratches that you may need to take care of. With long-term rentals, a lot of these minor issues need to be taken care of by the tenant, but this is not the case with short-term rentals.

Fewer Tenant Screening Options

With a short-term rental, the primary goal is to get as many people in and out quickly as possible. That is how you are going to make the most money. However, this does mean you do not have the opportunity to screen your tenants as you would in a long-term rental. At the start of your short-term rental endeavor, you may accept any potential guest who wants to book with you just so you can make some money and get some reviews on the rental platforms.

Some screening and security measures have been implemented with platforms such as Airbnb and VRBO. However, this is not a comprehensive screening process. It verifies basic information like a phone number, email address, and government ID. Then, there are reviews on the platform that you can check out. Just as a guest can rate and review you on the platform, the people who own the properties can write and review those who stay with them. It is always a good idea to look at these ratings and reviews to ensure that the person hasn't been destructive or inconsiderate. However, in many cases, the person may not have reviews, which means you won't have those to rely on when accepting their booking. There is always a chance that you will get a problematic guest who could cause damage to the property and violate the house rules you have set up.

INTERACTIVE ELEMENT: ARE SHORT-TERM RENTALS FOR YOU?

If you are considering the short-term rental option, then it is good to understand whether the pros outweigh the cons for you. The best way to do this is to note the cons and see how you can navigate them. Write down the cons you are most concerned about and then come up with one or two ideas that will mitigate the risks of those cons.

_____

_____

_____

_____

_____

Short-term rentals are important to consider as a real estate investment strategy. They can make you a steady income and help you reach financial freedom. One way to operate short-term rentals is through Airbnb. We will be discussing Airbnb as an investment strategy in more detail in the next chapter.

THE AIRBNB OPPORTUNITY

Out of all these short-term rental platforms out there, Airbnb is definitely the most popular and has the furthest reach. Like many other short-term rental property sites, Airbnb is essentially designed like a marketplace. This marketplace connects people looking for accommodation with people renting out their property on a short-term basis. It has created a way for people to make additional money, and it helps people looking for a vacation find unique places at a cheaper price.

It is fairly easy to sign up on the platform. Once you have created an account and uploaded all the relevant information, you can post your listing. From here, people will be able to view your listing when they are looking for a vacation rental in the area. You have full control of when you want to rent out your property and have access to a calendar where you can open up or block out specific dates. You will also be able to chat with people who are interested in renting out your property.

Airbnb also allows you to advertise unique stays and experiences. If there is something extra special about your property or it can offer an uncommon experience, then you'll be able to advertise this as something separate. For example, if you have access to horse riding or boating cruises, you could advertise these on the platform, too.

I have written books on Airbnb and short-term rentals that could help you gain further insights into the topic. There are lots of details and information that need to be considered when you are working through a platform like Airbnb. Not to mention the tips, tricks, and hacks you can use to increase your revenue and ensure the process is as smooth as possible. If this interests you, I highly suggest you pick up one of my other books so you can set yourself up for success when it comes to your Airbnb or short-term rental.

Before diving into this topic, it is important to take into account the legal regulations surrounding Airbnb. You don't want to pay any unnecessary fees or penalties down the road. As an Airbnb host, it is really important that you understand the laws in your city, country, state, or territory. You will need to get this advice directly from your government or municipality and keep checking back regularly for any changes. You can also check the Airbnb help center, which should offer some guidance for your city. You should also visit your local government website to see the permits or licenses needed to start a short-term rental business. Some things to look into are business licenses, building codes, zoning rules, permits, tax laws, and landlord-tenant laws. With that being said, let's go through some of the basics when it comes to using Airbnb.

Creating an Airbnb Account

The great thing about Airbnb is that it is incredibly easy to create an account. First, you will need to log onto the Airbnb website and choose the sign-up option. You will be guided step-by-step through the process by the use of prompts and forms.

In order to have an active Airbnb account, you will need to verify your account, and this usually requires your government-issued ID. You also need to upload a photo for facial recognition. Once you have done that, you will have to wait up to twenty-four hours for Airbnb to review and verify your information. Once you have done that, you will be approved on the Airbnb site and can continue to build your profile.

Listing a Property, Including Niche Options

There are many steps to take when listing a property on the Airbnb site. It is highly important that you do this properly because it is the only way that you get to market yourself on the website. When you first start listing your property, you must go through various steps to present the most accurate information. Remember, not all guests are looking for the same type of property or vacation, so being specific about what you have to offer is really important.

The first thing you must do to list your property is select your property type. There are different options for property types on the Airbnb website. Currently, the options are an apartment, house, self-contained unit, unique space, bed-and-breakfast, or boutique hotel. Have a look at your property and the space you offer and see which category suits it. You can rent out a room or even part of your home, so you are not just limited to the traditional versions of the above categories. Once you have selected your property type, you will then continue to get a little more specific. There are many options, including niche options. Whatever options you choose, just make sure that you are being honest and truthful because you want to manage your guest's expectations.

You will further categorize based on the type of space you will rent out. There are three options that you can choose from. The first is an entire home or apartment, which is pretty self-explanatory. With this option, you rent out the entire apartment or space for your guests to use. That means that any guest renting out the space will expect to have all the amenities you would find in a regular home or apartment. For example, they will look for things like a kitchen, laundry facilities, cooking utensils, and cleaning supplies. Think about a family or large group coming to stay for a while and what they would need. The next type is a shared room, which is when your guest will be sharing a room with another guest or guests. This is more like a hostel where multiple guests can stay together. The guest would expect to have shared amenities and rooms. Finally, you can have a private room where the guest would have their own private room or space, but other areas of the space will be shared with other people.

Once you have handled the type of property, you'll need to move on to selecting your location. Make sure your location is as accurate as possible because your guests will book primarily based on location. Your guests will not get your exact address until you have approved their stay and are in contact with them, but there will be a map that will give them a very general idea of where your property is.

You will need to specify how many bedrooms and bathrooms you have available, as well as the amenities. You will also need to indicate how many guests you will allow to book at once to ensure a comfortable stay.

You will then need to start taking some photos of your property to upload to the Airbnb website. This is highly important because people seek out potential vacation rentals with their eyes. If your pictures are eye-catching and interesting, then you will probably get more potential guests interested in your space. Ensure that you are taking clear pictures in good lighting. You can even get a professional photographer to assist you with getting excellent pictures of your property. You also want to ensure the property is neat and there is no unnecessary clutter when taking the pictures. Essentially, you want to put your best foot forward when you are snapping those pics.

Another important aspect of listing your property on the Airbnb website is creating a title and adding a description. The title will give anyone scrolling through the Airbnb listings a quick idea of what your property offers. Remember to choose your words carefully and be truthful. Once you've got your title, you can move on to creating a description, which is a lot more detailed. You can have a look at other Airbnb listings to get an idea of what descriptions work best. Make sure you supply a list of the features and benefits of your property. There is a rather large word count allotted for the description, so make sure you are being as detailed as possible.

At this point, your listing is almost ready to go, so you need to think about pricing. For a beginner, the best way to go about it is to do some research on similar Airbnb listings in your area to see what other people are charging. When you first start, you will need to price your rental competitively to get people to book with you. The more reviews you have and the more people who have stayed at your property, the easier it is going to be to find more guests. Remember to be realistic with your pricing and that you can always change it as time goes on. When you are more established, you can increase your nightly rate to be fairly compensated. Remember to also take into consideration things like the type of rental you have, the time of year, and your location. All of these will play a big role in your pricing strategy. It is a good idea to continuously do research and look at other Airbnb listings so you know how to price your property competitively.

It is good to note that you can save your listing without publishing it and come back and fill in the rest of the details later. Since it is a fairly comprehensive listing, it can take quite a long time, and you don't have to do it all in one sitting. Once you fill in all this information, you will need to answer some questions, and then you can publish your listing to the public. All that's left now is to watch the bookings roll in.

Setting Competitive Prices

I've already mentioned how important a competitive pricing strategy is. You will need to set yourself up for success, and you can do that by taking the right steps toward pricing your property correctly. First, you will want to figure out how much your Airbnb costs you per night. This is the base from where you will work out how much you are going to charge as a nightly rate. You should aim to make a profit or at least break even. Your nightly cost will need to include your rent, utilities, taxes, and any other costs that factor into running your Airbnb or owning your property. Since a lot of the bills and expenses are calculated on a monthly basis, you can simply take your monthly costs and divide them by thirty in order to get your nightly costs.

Now that you know exactly how much your Airbnb is costing you, it is time to think about how much profit you want to make. The rate you set should be higher than the nightly rate you spend on your Airbnb. You also have to take into consideration other things, such as the time you are spending to manage your Airbnb. This may not be a solid monetary value, but you are adding value to the guest and, therefore, need to charge for it. Make sure you do market research and look at how much other Airbnbs are charging for a similar service to what you offer. Even if you have decided on a price for your nightly rate, you need to adjust for the current market. If you are overcharging, it means people will not choose you as their first option. You are probably going to lose out on potential bookings because of this. If you are undercharging, it means that you are leaving money on the table and not optimizing your potential income.

Airbnb also has a smart pricing tool that you can either turn on or off. This tool will automatically shift your price up and down, depending on what is happening in the market. The algorithm will look at the demand for properties similar to yours and then determine a price to set per night. You can also set a minimum nightly rate that the smart pricing tool cannot go below so that you still have some control over your nightly rates. If you do not want to price your listing manually, then this is definitely a good option.

Managing Bookings Remotely

You may not be available to be at your property whenever guests check in and book with you. Perhaps you have multiple Airbnb properties, or maybe you are just not in town when you are going to have guests staying with you. Having a strategy to handle your bookings and guests remotely can give you much more flexibility when you are an Airbnb host.

COMMUNICATE WITH YOUR GUESTS

Communication is always going to be key when you are managing any kind of rental. Airbnb tracks how quickly you respond to your guests, and this shows up on your listing profile. It is even more important to prioritize communication with your guests if you will not be there in person to welcome them or have an in-person conversation with them.

You should focus on communicating with your guests before, during, and after check-in and their stay. You also want to make sure that you give your guests all the necessary information. You can also check in with your guests periodically throughout the day, depending on how long their stay is. You definitely don't want to overcommunicate while they stay on your property, as this can get highly annoying. Instead, check in on them once or twice, and then make sure you're easily reachable should they need you. Check in with them to see how they enjoyed their stay, and always ask if they are willing to give you a good review on the platform.

Set Up Automated Messaging

Life can get busy, so it is a good idea to set up some sort of automated message in case you cannot respond at a certain time. This message can be a welcome to your guests and provide them with all the information they need. You can also set up automatic replies to guest questions, which will help your guests get the answers they need without you having to be involved.

Set Plenty of Reminders

You will have many different responsibilities when you are an Airbnb host, so make sure to set reminders on your calendar so you do not get distracted or forget. If you have a guest checking in or you need to do maintenance on the property, set this in your calendar as a priority for you to do.

Solicit Guest Reviews

Solicitation sounds like a bad word, but it is important to always ask for a review. Sometimes, guests do forget, and getting good reviews bumps you up on the platform and puts you in a better position to find more potential guests. You can ask for a review a few days after your guests have checked out, and you can even send an automated message for this to happen. Remember to be polite when asking for a review, as this will increase your chances of getting a positive one.

Offer Self-Check-In

These days, a lot of technology is available to make a short-term rental owner's life easier. You can implement a self-check-in system so your guests can check in without you having to be there. This is a lot more convenient for both of you since you do not have to coordinate check-in times based on availability. One option for a self-check-in would be a lockbox where you leave the key to the property and give the guest a code to access the box. You can also change the property's locks to digital locks that open with a code, fingerprint, or password. You can then change this code or password for each guest, which is an additional level of security.

Get Home Security

Since you are welcoming people into your property, it is essential that you have a home security system. You will not be on the property often enough to make sure that it is safe and secure. You want to ensure your home is secure and your guests are safe. Installing security cameras and other security systems can be very helpful. If you are installing security cameras, be aware that Airbnb has strict rules surrounding the location of the cameras. They can be outside, but no cameras are allowed inside the home or property.

Make House Rules Clear

With Airbnb, you set the house rules, so make sure these are clear to your guests before they check in. You can send out the house rules to them in advance, but then also have a printed version of the house rules in the home. Some Airbnb hosts choose to put the relevant rules in the specific areas of the house. For example, if it is a non-smoking area, you can put up signs around the property to ensure that your guests know the rules and restrictions.

Compose a Guest Book

A guest book is a great way to show your guests that you care and provide them with all the information they need to enjoy their stay. This guest book can include things like instructions for the property and how-to manuals for the amenities and technology. You can also include the house rules as well as tips and tricks for enjoying their stay. Some Airbnb hosts go above and beyond and include local attractions and features in the area that guests may enjoy experiencing.

Organize a Welcome Gift

Another way to personalize your guest experience is to have a welcome gift ready for them when they check in. Since you will not be there in person, this is a nice touch that you can add to make a guest feel welcome. You can add whatever you want to this welcome pack, but making sure that it's on theme and will be useful to your guests is important. For example, you can include some local treats, important toiletries they may need, and even a friendly note for them.

Handling Guest Inquiries

One thing that will make your life so much easier is if you can anticipate your guests' questions and answer them before they even ask. That way, you do not have to go back and forth with questions and answers that could have easily been resolved from the get-go. On top of that, it is best to have your answers locked and loaded so you can give your guests accurate information if you are on the phone with them or communicating with them through email or on the Airbnb app. You can even have answers to common questions drafted out so you can simply copy and paste them, which makes it a lot easier. Below are a few of the most common questions that guests ask and some tips on how to answer them correctly.

Where Is the Property Located?

While the address will be given to your guests as soon as you accept them and they pay, it is still important to understand that some guests do not read all the details and may ask this question.

On top of the address, they will probably want to know how far it is from the amenities and the airport, as well as the directions from the airport to your property. You may also want to add some additional details on how to find your property, like the name of the building or any landmarks that could stand out to them.

Can We Check In or Out Early?

For the sake of convenience, some guests will ask if they can check in or out earlier or later than usual. Whether you accept earlier check-in or later check-out is up to you and is dependent on your schedule. If you have guests back to back, it might be difficult to accommodate these custom check-in and check-out times because you have to turn over the property and ensure it's clean and ready to go. If you cannot clean up and have the property ready for your next guest in a shorter amount of time, then it's best to let your guests know that you cannot accommodate a different check-in or check-out time. This is far better than letting them check into an untidy apartment or having the cleaning staff or you running up and down trying to get things ready while they are in the property. However, if you can accommodate them, your guests will appreciate it.

Does Your Property Have This Item?

Sometimes, guests will inquire about whether or not you have a certain item or amenity for them to use when they get to your property. To save time, you can have a list of all the items and amenities saved so you can easily send it to your guests or copy and paste this list into a message should they ask about a specific item. It is also a good idea to take as many pictures as possible of the important areas of your house so they can see what kinds of amenities and items are available.

What About a Discount?

You can't blame a guest for trying to get a discount so they can pay a little bit less. With that being said, you are under no obligation to give your guests a discount. However, you might consider selecting certain people to give discounts to under special circumstances. For example, if guests are staying for a longer time, you can offer a discount. You may also want to consider giving a discount to regular and loyal guests. Another good way to use a discount is to offer them at specific times of the year, like New Year celebrations, Christmas, or just when there is less demand in your area.

Can I Bring Someone Over, Such as a Family Member or a Friend?

Sometimes, a guest may want to invite other people over to the Airbnb once they have arrived. Sometimes, it is just for a visit, and others invite other people to stay with them. You should make sure that you are clear about your rules and policies surrounding the number of guests that are going to be on your property. Some guests want to have parties in the Airbnb, and this could get unruly and cause damage to your property. If you do not want parties in your Airbnb, then clearly state this in the rules. If you allow your guests to bring over other people, make sure they know the perimeters, such as how many guests can visit and when they need to leave.

Maintaining the Property

Maintenance is one of the most important things you can do for your property. When you run an Airbnb, it means there will be a lot of traffic in and out of your home. Maintenance is of the utmost importance because it shows that the house meets the standards your guests require and that you are not leaving things too

144 | CHAPTER 9

long before you start making fixes and changes. Having a schedule and list can help you stay on track with your maintenance. That way, you won't accidentally forget something.

Some things need to be done weekly. You will find a list of those things below.

- Inspect all plumbing and water sources for leaks.
- Wash windows and doors and inspect for cracks or damages.
- Double-check that all the locks in the house are working correctly.
- Check furniture.
- Check that all safety systems and fire extinguishers still work.
- Check for any indication of pests.
- Do a general clean and tidy up of the house.
- Test all remote controls and electronic devices.
- Check electrical outlets and light fixtures.
- Ensure all items are packed away where they need to be.

Becoming a Superhost

The title of Superhost is coveted among Airbnb hosts. Before we get into the rest of the topic, it is important to know what a Superhost is. A Superhost is somebody who has an above-average rating due to exceptional service and the provision of amazing guest experiences. When you get to Superhost status, you will get a badge displayed on your profile so that everybody can see it on the listing page. You can also charge a good amount more because you are reliable and now have an elevated status on the platform.

There are a few criteria that you need to meet in order to become a Superhost. The first criterion is that you have a minimum of three stays, which equals up to one hundred nights stayed, or a minimum of ten trips or reservations booked with you. You will also need to ensure that you keep the standard of a 90 percent response rate to potential guests who have questions or are looking to book with you. Your cancellation rate needs to be under one percent to show that you don't just cancel on your guests whenever you feel like it. Another incredibly important criterion is that you have a review score of 4.8 or more.

Once you have met all of these criteria, then you will be considered a Superhost. This is not something that you need to apply for. Instead, this is awarded automatically once you have met all the criteria. The review process takes place once every quarter, so you have a chance to be awarded a Superhost badge every three months. If, for any reason, you no longer meet the criteria, your badge will be removed, and you will need to work your way back up to being a Superhost.

INTERACTIVE ELEMENT: PLAN YOUR FIRST AIRBNB LISTING

Having a plan to start your very first Airbnb is so important. You must plan your listing and get everything in order before jumping in. I have written two books on becoming a successful Airbnb host. These could be essential reading should you want to become an Airbnb host.

You can find these by scanning the QR code below:

You can also get in touch with other people in the Airbnb community. More experienced people will be able to share a wealth of knowledge with you. I have created a Facebook group just for this purpose. I would encourage you to join and get an inside look at the world of Airbnb. Here are the details:

Name: Airbnb Host Community
URL: www.facebook.com/groups/airbnbhostcommunity
QR Code:

After exploring Airbnbs, it's now time to focus on long-term success and wealth-building strategies. In the next chapter, we will explore how to ensure sustainable growth and maximize your real estate investments over time.

LONG-TERM SUCCESS AND
WEALTH-BUILDING

"Real estate cannot be lost or stolen, nor can it be carried away. Purchased with common sense, paid for in full, and managed with reasonable care, it is about the safest investment in the world."

— FRANKLIN D. ROOSEVELT

PROPERTY REHAB

Property rehab is simply rehabilitating a property that may be in poor condition to make it live up to its full potential. You are essentially going to be restoring a piece of real estate to increase its functionality and appearance and raise the value of that property. There are many steps to consider when you do this, but it can be worth it if you do it right.

Property Condition Assessment

The first thing you will need to do is assess the property's current condition. This will give you a starting point so you can identify any big issues that need your attention. Ensure you do this assessment thoroughly and get professionals involved when necessary. You definitely don't want to be shocked by an enormous expense down the road.

Create a Checklist

Once you have done your assessments, you need to organize all of your information into a checklist. This will help you easily work through each thing that needs to be done for the renovation project. Doing this ensures that you understand the task at hand and keeps everything organized so you don't accidentally miss something.

Make a Budget

When it comes to real estate, everything costs money, so it is important to have a budget. Based on your checklist, try to figure out the estimated amount that you would need for each item. You also need to be prepared for emergencies and unforeseen expenses. Sometimes, you just don't know the full cost of something until you do it, so it is important to have some cushioning in your budget.

Find a Contractor

A good contractor will save you a lot of money but also a lot of time and stress. Choose a contractor with a lot of experience and a good track record. You also want to make sure the contractor you choose has experience with the type of renovations and improvements you are doing to your property.

Debris and Trash Removal

This is by no means the most glamorous part of the process, but you will need to organize the removal of any debris or trash on the property. This is not just for aesthetic purposes but for safety reasons as well. Accidents can happen if there are random items lying around. Depending on how much trash and debris is on the property, you may need to hire a service to assist you.

Interior Renovations

The most exciting part of any kind of rehabilitation or revamp of a property is probably the decorating, but you cannot start there. You first need to take care of structural issues and any other major problems before you move on to the design aspects. These are what's going to cost you the most money, and they may also be safety concerns. Dealing with this first is in the best interests of everybody who takes up residence on this property.

Work on the Exterior

The exterior of the house is also important because you want to increase curb appeal. The outside of the property is the first thing people see, so if you can draw them in from the get-go, you have a much better chance of increasing the value and getting people interested in either purchasing your property or renting it out from you. Take care of the lawn and exterior of the home and anything they can see from the street view.

Finalize the Project

Now is the time to do a walk-through to ensure all the work has been carried out to your liking. Don't simply trust your contractors or other people to approve everything. It is important for you to be involved in the finalizing process and make sure that you check everything thoroughly.

SELLING YOUR PROPERTY

There are many reasons why you may want to sell your property. It could be due to a life event, or it could be a strategic decision. There is no right or wrong answer to the question of when to sell your property, but you need to think about it before you do it. It is a big decision, and you want to make sure that you are thinking it through and considering all the options before you go through with the sale.

Below are some reasons why you might sell your property:

- In the case of a major life event, you may no longer be able to handle the maintenance or responsibility of the property.
- Your other investments bring in more income than this one.
- Your cap rate is sitting below the risk-free rate of return.
- You no longer find joy in owning this property but find it in something else that is more important to you.
- Other options may be more lucrative for your investments, and you want to explore those.
- The tax laws have changed, and now homeowners are getting stuck with excessive taxes.
- Your property is simply too expensive for you to handle at this moment.
- You no longer want to own this property for a personal reason.

As you can see, there are many reasons why somebody might not want to own a specific piece of property any longer. If you have considered it and examined all your options, it is perfectly okay to look into selling your property.

If you have decided that selling your property is the best way forward, it is important to think about ways to maximize your profit from the sale. One of the best ways to do this is to avoid as many taxes as possible when selling your property. There are various ways in which you can do that, and one way is through something called tax harvesting. In order to do this, you will be offsetting your capital gains with losses so that you can reduce the amount you are paying in tax. For example, if you see that your property has increased in value over the years, but you have other investments that have decreased in value, you can sell the other investments at a loss so you can balance out your overall capital gains and pay less tax. You could also use a 1031 exchange to reduce the amount you are paying in tax. As mentioned, you can use this exchange to purchase a similar property to avoid capital gains taxes. You could also use Section 121 exclusion, with which you can exclude up to a maximum amount of $500,000 if you are married and filing jointly on your capital gains. You can only do this by converting an investment property into your and your spouse's primary residence. If you are a single person, then this will be cut in half, and the benefit is $250,000.

When selling your rental property, there are other things to consider to increase the amount you will get from the sale. While considering capital gains tax is important, it's not the be-all and end-all. One of the best things you can do is to hire a professional who understands real estate investing and can help you through the process. This may result in you saving so much money in the long term that it will be worth it. You should also consider completing any repairs, renovations, or upgrades you had in the works. Even some repairs or renovations make a significant difference in the selling price of your property. You also need to ensure you are marketing your property well to attract buyers with money to spend. These are key to getting the price you deserve when you are selling your current real estate.

REINVESTING PROFITS

Once you have determined that selling your property is the best for you and you have received some profit, you need to decide what you will do with that profit. It may seem tempting for you to spend as much of it as possible. However, this is not usually the best way to go. Reinvesting that profit into other investment types is a much better long-term approach. You have already worked hard to build up your current real estate investment and make a profit, and you don't want to lose it by making a few bad purchasing decisions.

There are many things that you could invest your money into. With real estate, so many options are available that it is difficult to choose just one. Diversifying your investments is one of the best things you can do for the health of your future portfolio and to ensure you make the most profit possible. If you haven't already looked into a REIT, then this is the time to do so. This is a way that you can invest your money into real estate without being an active participant in managing your property. We have already done a deep dive into this kind of investment, so if you want a recap, it is best to go back to Chapter 1 and get all the information you need.

You can also diversify your investment portfolio through different types of real estate. If you have sold a property and are looking to invest in real estate differently, there are many categories you can look into. You can look into the geographical location of the properties you invest in. If all of your real estate investments are in one area, you can expand this by purchasing in a different city or even state. It does mean you will need to do some research on the state laws when it comes to real estate, but if you are willing to do that, you could make a very secure investment in a different geographical location.

You can also look at the type of properties that you are investing in and do something a little different. For example, if all of your property investments are long-term real estate investments, you can have a look at short-term rentals as an option. Different real estate investments will help you diversify your portfolio. You may also want to try a different investment strategy, such as house flipping or holding your investments for a longer time so they increase in value. Perhaps moving to a more active or passive investment is something that could also appeal to you, depending on your goals and what you have experienced in the past.

When you reinvest the money you have made through one of your investments, you are taking advantage of compounding your profits. You are essentially accelerating the growth of your wealth over time to increase it at an exponential rate. The more money you put into your investments, the more money you could potentially get out of it. This is why it is so important to think continuously about how to invest and get more out of your investments. The goal is to take advantage of the investment market so you can maximize your profits and ensure you are seeing the best returns possible.

WHY INFLATION IS AN ALLY

Whenever the topic of inflation is brought up, it typically has a negative connotation to it. This is understandable because when the price of things increases, your general profit may decrease since you are paying more money for the upkeep of your property. However, inflation can work to your benefit. When inflation hits, it means that the general prices of things increase, which also means that rent increases and the amount people will spend on properties will also increase. Essentially, you can charge a lot more rent or sell your property for more when experiencing higher inflation. This works best if you purchased your investment property when inflation was lower and the general price of things was also lower.

You can use inflation to your advantage when it comes to your real estate investment. One way is to focus on properties that generate a steady cash flow. When your real estate investments generate high cash flow, you can make more money when interest increases. If the prices of everything are already increasing, it means that you will probably be able to charge more rent on your properties and make more money. In this case, it might also be a good idea to go for short-term leases rather than longer-term ones. If you know that inflation will be a risk soon, you may want to lock in shorter-term leases so that you can increase the rent prices should inflation occur. If you and your tenant have a long-term lease, that means that you have to accept their rental payments at a fixed rate until the lease is terminated. A shorter-term lease means you can change the agreed-upon rental price based on factors such as inflation.

Diversifying your investment portfolio is a good way to protect yourself from interest rates. Diversification is incredibly important. You are investing, which means you are spreading out your investments and effectively lowering the risk you are facing. Where one investment may have a negative outlook when it comes to inflation, another investment might give you positive benefits when faced with inflation.

A huge part of being an investor is being knowledgeable about what is going on in the economy and the general market. While you can never fully predict what will happen with the economy, monitoring economic indicators is still a good idea. This way, you can prepare for any changes in the state of the economy. This may mean that you need to make different investments, sell your investments, or invest more heavily in what you currently are investing in. There will always be trends in the market, and staying aware and up-to-date with these will allow you to make better investment decisions. You can try to follow professionals on various social media platforms, newsletters, magazines, and other types of content. This will keep you in the loop with what is happening and help you be constantly notified when things are changing so you know what to expect. It is always better to be prepared rather than to be caught off guard.

INTERACTIVE ELEMENT: REFLECTION QUESTIONS

It is always important to reflect when it comes to your investment decisions. As you move through life, your investment choices will look different based on various factors. The goals you set five years ago might not be relevant now, and you will need to shift your goals and thought patterns to move into something better for the future. As you gain more experience in real estate investing, you may realize that your investment style changes, and so do the things you need and want. Ask the reflection questions below every once in a while so you can see where you stand when it comes to your investments:

- What are your long-term and short-term goals regarding your finances and real estate investing?
- How will you use real estate to help you reach your financial and personal goals?
- In which ways do you plan to diversify your investment portfolio?
- What strategy are you going to use to reinvest your profits from your current investments into future investments so you can build long-term wealth?

With a comprehensive understanding of long-term success strategies in real estate, you're now equipped to navigate the market confidently and build substantial wealth.

INSPIRE NEW INVESTORS TO GET STARTED!

You're about to begin one of the most exciting and rewarding ventures you've ever committed to—and this is your chance to inspire others and let them in on how to break into real estate investment.

Simply by sharing your honest opinion of this book and a little about your own story, you'll inspire new readers to take the plunge —and you'll show them exactly where they can find all the information they need to make a success of it.

LEAVE A REVIEW!

Thank you so much for your support. I wish you every success with your investments!

Scan the QR code below

CONCLUSION

Investing in real estate is one of the most rewarding journeys you can go on. It definitely takes a lot of work, but all the effort you will put in will be worth it. When you invest in real estate, you are also investing in your future. There is a reason so many people want to get into real estate. Now that you have reached the end of this book, you have all the tools you need to become a successful real estate investor. Just remember that all it takes is one small step at a time. You don't have to put pressure on yourself to become a multimillionaire in a matter of months. Taking a few small steps at a time is the best way to approach investing in real estate. Focus on one aspect first and then keep building on that momentum.

There are so many types of real estate out there that you can find one that suits your needs and financial goals. If you are a beginner investor and don't have a lot of funds to play with, then you can start small by investing in a real estate investment trust. This is a great place to start, so you can get a feel for investing in real estate without actually purchasing a property. From there, you can continuously build up and then take steps toward other types of real estate investments. As long as you have a plan and are taking action to stick to it, then you are on the right path. There is no one way to be a real estate investor, so it is up to you to create a strategy and a plan that is going to work for you and your finances. The power is completely in your hands, and you can tailor your investment strategy while using the principles in this book to help guide you.

You've learned the essentials of real estate investing, from financing and purchasing properties to managing short-term rentals and leveraging long-term strategies. Now, it's time to put these insights into action and start building your real estate empire!

If you have found this book helpful, I'd really appreciate it if you gave it a positive review on the platform where you purchased it. This will help to extend my reach and ensure more people are well-equipped for the fulfilling journey of investing in real estate. Don't forget to check out my other books as well!

GLOSSARY

1031 Exchange: This allows for tax to be deferred by selling a property and using that money to buy a new property without paying capital gains tax on the sale.

Amortization: An accounting method to spread loan payments over a certain time. The payments will cover the principal and interest.

ARM: Also known as adjustable-rate mortgage. With this type of loan, the interest rate adjusts or changes over time.

Amenity: This refers to an extra feature or appliance that a property has.

Appreciation: When the value of a property increases over time due to market demand, improvements, or inflation.

APR (Annual Percentage Rate): The yearly cost of a loan, including all additional fees and rates.

BRRRR: This refers to an investment strategy where you buy, rehab, rent, refinance, and repeat.

Cash Flow: The net amount being transferred in and out of an investment after income and expenses.

Cap Rate (Capitalization Rate): This is used to assess how profitable a real estate investment will be by dividing the NOI by the purchase price.

CMA: A comparative market analysis, which is a report on the market value of a property based on a comparison of similar properties in the same area.

Collateral: Pledging an asset for a loan so if you default on the loan, the lender can repossess it to get their money out.

Depreciation: The value of an asset decreases over time due to various factors.

Equity: The difference between the market value and the amount owed on the property.

Fair Market Value: The estimated price a property can be sold for on the current market.

HELOC: Also known as Home Equity Line of Credit, it allows a borrower to take out credit up to a certain limit by leveraging equity in a property they currently own.

Homeowners Association (HOA): An organization that manages the affairs and operations of a certain group of properties that are owned or rented by multiple different people.

HVAC: Heating, Ventilation, and Air Conditioning system.

Interest Rate: A percentage fee that is charged on a loan.

Leverage: To use a loan or credit to purchase a piece of real estate.

Liquidity: Signifies how quickly an asset can be sold or converted into cash.

LMI (Lenders Mortgage Insurance): Insurance that protects the lender if the borrower defaults on a loan.

LTV: This stands for loan-to-value ratio and is used to calculate the potential risk of a loan compared to the value of the property.

NOI: This stands for net operating income and indicates the income generated after subtracting the expenses.

Principal: The original amount of money borrowed, without the additional fees or interest.

REIT: Also known as a Real Estate Investment Trust. This entity pools together investment capital from multiple investors to purchase, operate, or finance properties to generate investment returns.

ROI (Return on Investment): Evaluates the profitability of an investment. This is calculated by dividing the net profit by the investment cost.

REFERENCES

"3 Highly Motivational Real Estate Success Stories - New Silver," January 25, 2024. https://newsilver.com/the-lender/real-estate-success-stories/.

"7 Pros and Cons of Owning a Short Term Rental | Short Term Rental Manager," April 20, 2018. https://shorttermrentalmanager.com/7-pros-and-cons-of-owning-a-short-term-rental/.

"10 Common Rental Property Repairs Landlords Need to Know About | Travelers Insurance," November 14, 2022. https://www.travelers.com/resources/home/landlords/10-common-rental-property-repairs-landlords-need-to-know-about.

"20 Expert Tips for Successfully Managing an Airbnb Remotely." https://awning.com/post/manage-airbnb-remotely.

"50 Questions To Ask Before Investing in Real Estate." https://www.linkedin.com/pulse/50-questions-ask-before-investing-real-estate-camaplan.

Admin. "Land Investing - How To Make Money in 9 Steps." *Best Real Estate Investment Company in Lekki, Lagos, Nigeria* (blog), May 16, 2022. https://eystone.ng/land-investing/.

Guest Author. "How and Why You Need to Diversify Your Real Estate Portfolio - Stessa." https://www.stessa.com/blog/how-and-why-you-need-to-diversify-your-real-estate-portfolio/.

Booking Ninjas. "What Is a Residential Property? Types, Features, and Benefits." https://www.bookingninjas.com/blog/what-is-a-residential-property-types-features-and-benefits.

Brown, Jerry. "27 Loan Terminologies You Must Know." Forbes Advisor, February 9, 2021. https://www.forbes.com/advisor/personal-loans/loan-terminologies/.

Cain, Sarah Li. "10 Key Questions To Ask When Buying A House." Bankrate, July 17, 2024. https://www.bankrate.com/real-estate/questions-to-ask-when-buying-a-house/.

Contributor, Guest. "8 Strategies for Real Estate Investing During Inflation." REtipster, August 3, 2023. https://retipster.com/8-strategies-for-real-estate-investing-during-inflation/.

DeAngelo, Nic. "Understanding Compounding in Real Estate." *Saint Investment* (blog), September 28, 2023. https://saintinvestment.com/blog/understanding-compounding-in-real-estate/.

Dieker, Nicole. "Why Is Good Credit So Important?" Bankrate, November 3, 2023. https://www.bankrate.com/credit-cards/advice/why-is-good-credit-so-impor tant/.

Drake Law. "Key Legal Factors to Consider Before Investing in Real Estate." https://www.drakelaw.ca/legal-insights/key-legal-factors-to-consider-before-investing-in-real-estate.

Elphick, Dean. "Airbnb Superhost: How to Become a Superhost on Airbnb." Little Hotelier, October 10, 2022. https://www.littlehotelier.com/blog/get-more-bookings/airbnb-superhost/.

Ferran. "10 Ways To Make More Money From Rental Properties." *June Homes Blog* (blog), January 23, 2024. https://junehomes.com/blog/2024/01/23/make-more-money-from-rental-properties/.

Fettke, Kathy. "Top 60 Real Estate Definitions for Investors to Know." *RealWealth* (blog). https://realwealth.com/learn/real-estate-definitions/.

FortuneBuilders. "House Hacking: A Beginner's Guide," September 21, 2022. https://www.fortunebuilders.com/p/what-is-house-hacking/.

Griggs Homes. "What Is Property Development and How Does It Work?" https://www.griggshomes.co.uk/what-is-property-development-how-does-it-work.

Hamed, Eman. "The Complete Beginner's Guide to Investing in Long-Term Rentals." *Learn Real Estate Investing | Mashvisor Real Estate Blog* (blog), March 7, 2019. https://www.mashvisor.com/blog/beginners-guide-long-term-rentals/.

Harrington, Dennis. "The Rise of Renters by Choice." Multifamily Executive, May 18, 2022. https://www.multifamilyexecutive.com/property-management/demo graphics/the-rise-of-renters-by-choice_o.

"Highlights From the Profile of Home Buyers and Sellers," November 13, 2023. https://www.nar.realtor/research-and-statistics/research-reports/highlights-from-the-profile-of-home-buyers-and-sellers.

"How Much Should I Charge for Rent: Tips to Rental Rates." https://www.mysmart move.com/blog/how-much-charge-for-rent.

https://prenohq.com/. "How to Start an Airbnb: A Beginners Guide." https://prenohq.com/blog/how-to-list-your-property-on-airbnb/.

Investopedia. "5 Negotiating Strategies When Selling Your Home." https://www.investopedia.com/articles/mortgages-real-estate/12/playing-hardball-when-selling-your-home.asp.

Investopedia. "Calculating Net Operating Income (NOI) for Real Estate." https://www.investopedia.com/terms/n/noi.asp.

Investopedia. "Capitalization Rate: Cap Rate Defined With Formula and Examples." https://www.investopedia.com/terms/c/capitalizationrate.asp.

Investopedia. "Commercial Real Estate: Definition and Types." https://www.investopedia.com/terms/c/commercialrealestate.asp.

Investopedia. "Fixed-Rate Mortgage: How It Works, Types, vs. Adjustable Rate." https://www.investopedia.com/terms/f/fixed-rate_mortgage.asp.

Investopedia. "How Airbnb Works—for Hosts, Guests, and the Company Itself." https://www.investopedia.com/articles/personal-finance/032814/pros-and-cons-using-airbnb.asp.

Investopedia. "How to Profit From Inflation." https://www.investopedia.com/articles/investing/080813/how-profit-inflation.asp.

Investopedia. "Interest-Only Mortgage: Definition, How They Work, Pros and Cons." https://www.investopedia.com/terms/i/interestonlymortgage.asp.

Investopedia. "Loan Terms: Specific Terms Defined and How to Negotiate Them." https://www.investopedia.com/loan-terms-5075341.

Investopedia. "REIT: What It Is and How To Invest." https://www.investopedia.com/terms/r/reit.asp.

Investopedia. "Rent-to-Own Homes: How the Process Works." https://www.investopedia.com/updates/rent-to-own-homes/.

Investopedia. "Residential Rental Property Definition, Tax Pros & Cons." https://www.investopedia.com/terms/r/residentialrentalproperty.asp.

Investopedia. "What Is a 1031 Exchange? Know the Rules." https://www.investopedia.com/financial-edge/0110/10-things-to-know-about-1031-exchanges.aspx.

Investopedia. "What Is Comparative Market Analysis (CMA) in Real Estate?" https://www.investopedia.com/terms/c/comparative-market-analysis.asp.

Investopedia. "What You Should Know About Real Estate Valuation." https://www.investopedia.com/articles/realestate/12/real-estate-valuation.asp.

"Key Financial Metrics for Real Estate Investors | Cg Tax, Audit & Advisory," October 24, 2023. https://www.cgteam.com/key-financial-metrics-for-real-estate-investors/.

Landon, Dena. "The Top 10 Metrics Every Real Estate Investor Should Know (and Why) - Stessa." https://www.stessa.com/blog/10-real-estate-investing-metrics/.

Lodgify. "All About Short-Term Rentals," n.d. https://www.lodgify.com/guides/business/short-term/.

Lodgify. "What Is a Vacation Rental?" n.d. https://www.lodgify.com/encyclopedia/vacation-rental/.

Mann (Silvermann), Baruch. "How Does Inflation Affect Real Estate? Here's What You Need to Know." Entrepreneur, December 2, 2022. https://www.entrepreneur.com/money-finance/how-does-inflation-affect-real-estate-heres-what-you-need/433953.

Marketing. "Giving Rehab Property a Makeover: A Real Estate Investor's Guide." Reedy & Company, December 7, 2023. https://www.reedyandcompany.com/blog/giving-rehab-property-a-makeover-a-real-estate-investors-guide/.

Martin, Allison. "Cash-Out Refinancing: What It Is, How It Works." Bankrate, September 5, 2024. https://www.bankrate.com/mortgages/cash-out-refinanc ing/.

McCracken, Madison. "The Importance of Thorough Tenant Screening Process." *Bay Property Management Group* (blog), April 6, 2022. https://www.baymgmt group.com/blog/tenant-screening/.

Memphis Investment Properties. "7 Benefits of Owning a Rental Property," November 8, 2021. https://www.memphisinvestmentproperties.net/7-benefits-of-owning-a-rental-property/.

NerdWallet. "How to Buy a House: 15 Steps in the Homebuying Process," March 19, 2024. https://www.nerdwallet.com/article/mortgages/home-buying-check list-steps-to-buying-house.

NerdWallet. "How to Get Preapproved for a Mortgage," April 25, 2024. https://www.nerdwallet.com/article/mortgages/how-to-get-a-mortgage-preapproval.

New Western. "Marketing Your Investment: Step-by-Step Guide on Selling Your Investment Property Like the Pros." https://www.newwestern.com/guide/sell ing-a-rental-property/.

Newsroom. "Airbnb Q4-2023 and Full-Year Financial Results." Airbnb, February 13, 2024. https://news.airbnb.com/airbnb-q4-2023-and-full-year-financial-results/.

Oak, Red. "Top 7 Reasons Why 90% of US Millionaires Invest In Real Estate & Why You Should Follow the Lead." *Red Oak Development Group* (blog), August 3, 2022. https://redoakvc.com/top-7-reasons-why-90-of-us-millionaires-invest-in-real-estate-why-you-should-follow-the-lead/.

Ostrowski, Jeff. "What Is A HELOC (Home Equity Line Of Credit)?" Bankrate, April 24, 2024. https://www.bankrate.com/home-equity/what-is-heloc/.

Passive Real Estate Investing. "From Zero to 35 Rentals in 4 Years – A Client Success Story," January 30, 2018. https://www.passiverealestateinvesting.com/from-zero-to-35-rentals-in-4-years-a-client-success-story/.

Rajkhar. "Tax Saving by Investing in Real Estate." Reddit, 2024. https://www.reddit.com/r/realestateinvesting/comments/1blsscr/tax_saving_by_invest ing_in_real_estate/.

"Real Estate Risks: What It Is and How to Avoid Them." https://www.mandanibay.com/blog/risks-of-real-estate-investment-and-how-to-avoid-them/.

Richards, Laurie. "What Is A Balloon Mortgage And Why Is It Risky?" Bankrate, July 15, 2024. https://www.bankrate.com/mortgages/what-is-a-balloon-mort gage/.

Rocket Mortgage. "Lease Option: Definition And How It Works." https://www.rocketmortgage.com/learn/lease-option.

Rocket Mortgage. "Seller Financing: How It Works, Pros And Cons And If It's A Good Idea." https://www.rocketmortgage.com/learn/seller-financing.

Rocket Mortgage. "Top 6 Tax Benefits Of Real Estate Investing." https://www.rocketmortgage.com/learn/tax-benefits-of-real-estate-investing.

Rocket Mortgage. "Understanding The BRRRR Method Of Real Estate Investment." https://www.rocketmortgage.com/learn/brrrr.

Rodriguez, Amanda. "Understanding NOI/Cap Rate & How to Calculate Them." *Learn Real Estate Investing | Mashvisor Real Estate Blog* (blog), July 10, 2023. https://www.mashvisor.com/blog/noi-cap-rate/.

Rohde, Jeff. "What Is Due Diligence in Real Estate? A Simple Guide and Checklist." https://learn.roofstock.com/blog/what-is-due-diligence-in-real-estate.

Samurai, Financial. "When To Sell An Investment Property: Every Indicator To Consider." *Financial Samurai* (blog), August 17, 2019. https://www.financialsamurai.com/when-to-sell-an-investment-property/.

"Self-Management vs. Property Company: Which Is Better? | BiggerPockets Blog," May 12, 2023. https://www.biggerpockets.com/blog/property-management-vs-self-management.

Sharkey, Sarah. "Putting A Down Payment On Investment Property: What To Know." Quicken Loans, October 20, 2023. https://www.quickenloans.com/learn/down-payment-on-investment-property.

Strategies for Influence. 2019. "Robert Kiyosaki - Rich Dad Poor Dad." Strategies for Influence. November 17, 2019. https://strategiesforinfluence.com/robert-kiyosaki-rich-dad-poor-dad/.

"Successfully Estimating Renovation Costs in Real Estate." https://www.dealmachine.com/blog/successfully-estimating-renovation-costs-in-real-estate.

Team, BnB Hosts. "How to Handle The Most Common Airbnb Guest Enquiries Like a Pro." *BnB Hosts* (blog), September 24, 2019. https://www.bnbhosts.com.au/common-airbnb-enquiries/.

"The 7 Best Short Term Rental Sites | Uplisting.Io." https://www.uplisting.io/blog/the-7-best-short-term-rental-sites-for-hosts.

The Balance. "How You Can Build (or Lose) Equity in Your Home." https://www.thebalancemoney.com/definition-of-equity-1798546.

"The Ultimate 35-Point House Rehab Checklist." https://www.theinvestorsedge.com/blog/the-ultimate-36-point-house-rehab-checklist.

"The Ultimate Airbnb Maintenance Checklist and Schedule | Minut." https://www.minut.com/blog/airbnb-maintenance-checklist-and-schedule.

Todd, Jonny. "Viewing a House Checklist: Key Questions to Ask When Buying." Ellis & Co, July 26, 2022. https://www.ellisandco.co.uk/guides/buying/viewing-a-house-checklist-8457/.

Tom. "How to Get Your Airbnb Pricing Strategies Right: 7 Steps." *Host Tools* (blog), July 24, 2020. https://hosttools.com/blog/short-term-rental-tips/airbnb-pric ing-strategies/.

Tross, Kasey. "The 6 Types of Commercial Real Estate Property." *VTS* (blog), May 8, 2023. https://www.vts.com/blog/the-6-types-of-commercial-real-estate-prop erties.

TRVLGUIDES [Learn How To Travel]. "How To Create An Airbnb Account [Or Change Or Delete It]." https://trvlguides.com/articles/create-airbnb-account.

Ugazu, Yassine. "Glossary of Real Estate & Vacation Rental Investing Terms." *Learn Real Estate Investing | Mashvisor Real Estate Blog* (blog), August 24, 2023. https:// www.mashvisor.com/blog/real-estate-investing-terms/.

Wall Street Prep. "Net Operating Income (NOI) | Formula + Calculator." https:// www.wallstreetprep.com/knowledge/noi-net-operating-income/.

"What Is a Variable Rate Mortgage and How Do They Work | L&C." https://www. landc.co.uk/mortgage-guides/variable-rate-mortgage.

"What Is the Due Diligence Period in Real Estate? - Experian," November 4, 2022. https://www.experian.com/blogs/ask-experian/what-is-due-diligence-period- real-estate/.

"What Is Real Estate Appreciation?" https://smartasset.com/investing/real-estate- appreciation.

"What Is Underwriting In Real Estate? Full Guide." https://www.metawealth.co/ post/what-is-underwriting-in-real-estate-explained.

"What's a REIT (Real Estate Investment Trust)?" https://www.reit.com/what-reit.

Wieland, David. "Council Post: Assessing Three Types Of Risk In Real Estate." Forbes. https://www.forbes.com/councils/forbesrealestatecouncil/2020/08/ 05/assessing-three-types-of-risk-in-real-estate/.

Yale, Laura Grace Tarpley, CEPF, Aly J. "Saving for a Down Payment: Strategies to Achieve Homeownership." Business Insider. https://www.businessinsider.com/ personal-finance/mortgages/tips-for-saving-for-a-down-payment.

"Your Essential Guide to Navigating Real Estate & Your Credit," July 27, 2023. https://mathesonattys.com/blog/real-estate-and-your-credit/.

Yuhenyo. "Property Is Severely Under Valued by Potential Lender Bank." Reddit, 2023. https://www.reddit.com/r/AusPropertyChat/comments/180asha/proper ty_is_severely_under_valued_by_potential/.

Zillow. "75% of Recent Home Buyers Have Regrets about Their New Home." https://www.prnewswire.com/news-releases/75-of-recent-home-buyers-have- regrets-about-their-new-home-301477283.html.

Zinn, Dori. "Flipping Houses: A How-To Guide For Beginners." Bankrate, July 8, 2024. https://www.bankrate.com/real-estate/flipping-houses/.

IMAGE REFERENCES

BP, Steve. *Calculator, Calculation, Insurance Image.* July 9, 2014. Photograph. https://pixabay.com/photos/calculator-calculation-insurance-385506/.

Kuhar, Milivoj. *Man Climbing on Ladder Inside Room.* February 2, 2018. Image. https://unsplash.com/photos/man-climbing-on-ladder-inside-room-Te48TPzdcU8.

Li, Kostiantyn. *A House Made out of Money on a White Background.* October 20, 2021. Image. https://unsplash.com/photos/a-house-made-out-of-money-on-a-white-background-1sCXwVoqKAw.

Mallorca, Tierra. *White and Red Wooden House Miniature on Brown Table.* June 14, 2019. Photograph. https://unsplash.com/photos/white-and-red-wooden-house-miniature-on-brown-table-rgJ1J8SDEAY.

Tingey Injury Law Firm. *A Wooden Gavel on a White Marble Backdrop.* May 13, 2020. Photograph. https://unsplash.com/photos/brown-wooden-smoking-pipe-on-white-surface-6sl88x150Xs.

Wheeler, Blake. *Housing Development American Fork.* April 4, 2017. Photograph. https://unsplash.com/photos/aerial-photography-houses-zBHU08hdzhY.

THE ULTIMATE HOUSE FLIPPING AND BRRRR REAL ESTATE INVESTING BEGINNER'S BOOK

BUILD WEALTH THROUGH FIX-AND-FLIP AND THE BUY, REHAB, RENT, REFINANCE, REPEAT STRATEGY—EVEN IF YOU'RE ON A TIGHT BUDGET

INTRODUCTION

Financial freedom is the goal, right? I don't think there are many people out there who wouldn't want financial freedom in their lives, where they can say they have built up enough wealth so that finances are not a huge source of stress for them. There are many people who claim to have found the answer to financial freedom with their hacks and business ideas, but the truth is that real estate is one of the most solid investments to ensure financial freedom and wealth building.

Real estate is one of the longest-standing investments available. If you talk to members of the older generation, you will quickly discover that many of them are advocates of investing in real estate. This is because, in general, the return on investment in real estate far outperforms many other traditional investments over the long run. Even though stocks and bonds are good investments, real estate tends to perform better than those. It is one of the most stable, trustworthy, and rewarding investments available.

You might be one of the people who feel that real estate investing is either out of reach or very intimidating. If this is the case, that is okay because you are not alone. We all start somewhere. The truth is, I was definitely apprehensive when it came to real estate investing and whether it was a good option. I only started investing in real estate out of necessity because I needed somewhere to live, and I didn't have much money to pay for it. As a new immigrant family, we didn't have all the resources in the world. The only thing I could afford was an old, broken-down house, but I was willing to put in the work. After a few years of renovating, I refinanced the house, and it was worth much more than I had paid for it. The cash-out I received from refinancing was used to access the equity in my house and put a down payment on a two-bedroom apartment. I used it to start my short-term rental business, and my real estate investment journey began. I know it can be intimidating to start, but I was able to do it, and now I want to help others create the same for themselves.

Before we get ahead of ourselves, let's take some time to define what real estate investing is. Real estate is property that can include land and anything that is permanently attached to or built on it. Typically, real estate is divided into five main categories: commercial, residential, industrial, raw land, and special use land. You can invest in any one of these types, but as a first-time or beginner investor, residential tends to be the better option because it is more accessible and requires less specialized knowledge. When you invest in real estate, you are purchasing the property, land, or home. Then you can either rent or sell the property to make a profit. This is a very simple breakdown of what real estate investing is, as there are many different strategies that fall under this umbrella. The two main strategies we are going to focus on in this book are house flipping and the BRRRR (Buy, Rehab, Rent, Refinance, Repeat) method. We will be diving more into both of these in this book, but let's give you an overview of the BRRRR method. This is a strategy where you buy a property that might need a bit of work and renovate it to increase its value. Then you rent it out for additional income and eventually refinance the property to access equity to fund your next investment property. If this all sounds like another language, don't worry, we are going to cover this and house flipping to help you along your journey. The important thing to know is that both are great strategies to help build your wealth as a beginner real estate investor and see significant gains with your investments.

There are many myths surrounding real estate investing, which discourage a lot of people from even giving it a try. I want to put these myths to rest. You don't need to be wealthy to start investing, nor do you need to be a landlord, own a house, or time the market perfectly. At the end of the day, all you need to do is be willing to start and ensure that you are taking the right steps to reach your goal. While there are risks involved in investing in real estate, the truth is that any investment carries some level of risk. As the saying goes, "no risk, no reward." However, you must do your best to mitigate these risks and ensure that you are not making rushed decisions. It is important to understand that sometimes we need to take a step in the right direction for things to work out. There are numerous success stories of people who started investing in real estate and have now seen significant returns on their investments. You can be one of those success stories, too.

In this book, we will go through a three-part framework that outlines the key elements for investing in real estate through house flipping and the BRRRR method. The first part is the foundational section of the book, where we will learn about the two main strategies we will discuss. Then we will move on to part two, which focuses on taking action and making the right moves to find, fix, rent, or sell the property. The final part, part three, will dive into building smart and growing big. In this section, we will discuss how to grow your investment and ensure that you are making smart decisions to protect yourself and your investment.

My hope for you is that by the end of this book, you will have the confidence to start investing in real estate using your chosen strategy. Both house flipping and the BRRRR method are great ways to begin your real estate investment journey, but it is important to understand what they are and what your first step should be. So, without any further delay, let's dive into Chapter 1, where we will discuss these strategies.

PART I

LEARN THE STRATEGIES

FLIP VS. BRRRR—WHICH ONE'S RIGHT FOR YOU?

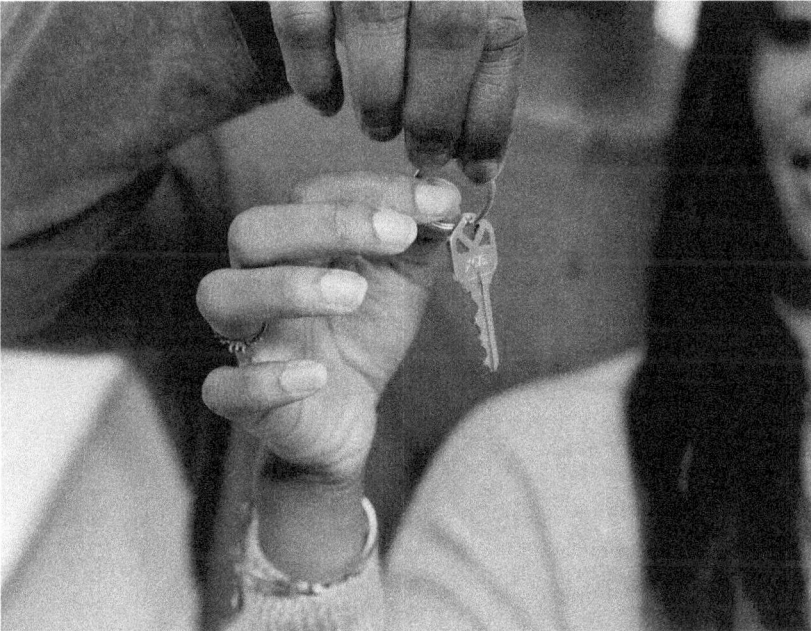

I n 2024, the US real estate market saw a notable shift: While traditional home sales faced challenges, investors found opportunities in alternative strategies. Notably, 41% of residential real estate investors reported higher earnings compared to the previous year (Pisano 2024). These figures highlight the potential of informed investment choices.

UNDERSTANDING HOUSE FLIPPING AND THE BRRRR STRATEGY

You may or may not have heard of house flipping before, but I am sure that you have watched a TV show where someone buys houses and renovates them. After the renovations are completed, they sell the house and make a profit. This is the basic principle of house flipping. When someone wants to flip a house, they must conduct extensive research to find a property within a reasonable price range. Then, they will assess what needs to be done to improve the value of the home. This could involve larger projects, such as adding an extra bedroom or bathroom, or removing the entire floor and replacing it with something more modern, durable, and functional. It could also include smaller tasks like repainting, refurnishing, and adding new finishes to the existing amenities and furniture.

Unlike many other real estate investment strategies, when you flip a house, the goal is to make a profit as soon as possible. Remember that a property is a significant investment, and if you are going to put a lot of money into it, you also want to ensure that you can recoup your investment as quickly as possible. Many people who invest in house flipping aim to flip houses frequently so that they can consistently achieve a good return on their investments. If done correctly, flipping houses can be a highly effective investment strategy that yields substantial profits. In fact, in 2024, house flipping generated a median profit of $73,500 per property (Gratton 2025a). That is an impressive return on investment for a strategy that allows you to access your profits relatively quickly after making the investment.

But before you pick up your drill and paintbrush, you need to be aware of the main aspects that lead to house-flipping success. It's not as easy as simply making a property attractive and then selling it off. You will first need to consider the overall market appreciation in the neighborhood where you are going to purchase your property. The truth is that some neighborhoods are better than others when it comes to investing. If a neighborhood has a bad reputation, lacks amenities, or is unsafe or difficult to navigate, then the likelihood of making a good profit is quite slim. People will always prefer to pay a little more to live in a better area, even if the property is smaller than what they would have gotten in a less desirable area.

Another important factor to consider is how much value the improvements will add to the property. You'll need to carefully evaluate which improvements to make based on what will add the most value and, therefore, yield the most profit. Some improvements are merely nice to have; they may enhance the property's appearance or feel, but they do not significantly increase its value when you are trying to resell. Since the goal of property flipping is to maximize profit, it is important to consider which types of renovations and improvements will generate income and which ones may not be worth the investment.

Let's shift gears and discuss something that is often mistaken for house flipping but can be considered a level up from traditional house flipping. It is called the BRRRR method, which stands for Buy, Rehab, Rent, Refinance, and Repeat. The goal is to purchase distressed properties, fix them up, rent them out, and generate income from them. While this is happening, you are building equity, which you can then use toward your next property. Unlike house flipping, you retain possession of the property because you are renting it out for income rather than selling it. This way, it is not a one-time profit but rather a source of income over a longer timeframe.

In order for this method to work, an investor will need to make sure they can make enough money through their rent to cover the mortgage. If they are only able to rent out the property for less than the amount they have to pay on their monthly mortgage payments, it means that they will not be making a profit, and this investment is going to be a losing battle.

In order to almost guarantee that you will make a good profit from this method, you need to ensure that you are purchasing a property at a discounted price. The cheaper you can buy a property, the more potential you have to make a larger profit. With that said, you must conduct thorough research to ensure that the area, as well as other factors, will work in your favor. There is no point in purchasing a property that is cheap if it has absolutely nothing else going for it. We will dive deeper into the BRRRR method in Chapter 5, so stay tuned for an in-depth exploration of the method later in the book.

For now, let's discuss some of the numbers you might expect in a successful BRRRR deal (Blankenship 2023b). Let's say you have a property that you are looking to purchase, and it costs $100,000. The closing costs are $5,000, with the rehab costs being around $25,000. All in all, this means that the total cost for which you will need to secure a loan would be $130,000. The monthly rent is $1,200, which means that the annual rent taken in would be $14,400. After you have completed all of the renovations, the new value of the property is $180,000, and your new loan amount, which is 80% of the appraised value, is $144,000. This means your cash pullout would be $14,000.

The new monthly mortgage payment, with a 4% interest rate over 30 years, would be $687. Now you have $14,000 freed up, which you can use as the down payment on another property, allowing you to repeat the BRRRR method. If the monthly mortgage payment is $687 and the monthly rent you will be charging is $1,200, it means that you are making a significant profit that you can reinvest into the mortgage or use to finance another property, depending on what works best for you. This is how the BRRRR method operates in real life.

PROS AND CONS

As you can probably tell, there are some definite similarities between house flipping and the BRRRR method. While those similarities are important, it is even more crucial to note the differences when deciding which method you will use to build your property investment portfolio. Both strategies start by acquiring an undervalued property and then renovating it to increase its value. The difference lies in the exit strategy: House flipping focuses on selling the property as quickly as possible to make a profit, while the BRRRR method emphasizes renting out the property and creating equity so you can continue investing.

House Flipping

Pros

With house flipping, there are plenty of pros that make it attractive to many investors. One of the most appealing aspects is the potential for a quick profit. When a house flip is done correctly, you can achieve faster returns on your investment compared to most other real estate strategies. Once your house is on the market and sold, you will receive almost immediate profits from it. The goal of

184 | CHAPTER 1

house flipping is to renovate and sell the house as soon as possible to secure these quick profits. Additionally, as a house flipper, you will be improving a property's value through upgrades and renovations, allowing you to see the value you are creating on the property as it unfolds.

You will also begin to gain a wealth of market knowledge simply by the nature of house flipping. You will be buying and selling properties quite often, which means you will develop a better understanding of the real estate market in your local area. This knowledge is invaluable as you continue your real estate investment journey. If you are investing in real estate in other ways, choosing house flipping can be a great way to diversify your current portfolio. You can expand your portfolio and increase your potential profit by engaging in something a little different and more hands-on.

Cons

One of the biggest potential downsides to house flipping is the risk of significant financial losses due to unforeseen problems or inadequate research conducted prior to purchasing the property. When it comes to any form of real estate investing, some risk is always involved; therefore, it is crucial to understand what you are getting into before you jump in. Additionally, house flipping is resource- and time-intensive, which means it requires a considerable amount of work as well as a substantial financial investment.

In addition to the money and resources needed to complete a house-flipping project, you must also consider the time commitment and the potential stress of the process. As an investor, you will need to be present every step of the way as the property undergoes renovation. This is essential to ensure that everything runs smoothly, and if any issues arise, you will need to be there to address them to achieve the desired outcome. If you have ever undertaken any building project, you know that unexpected challenges can arise, and many aspects may not go according to plan. This can be highly stressful and may require more resources, time, and money than you initially anticipated. This is why it is so important to be resilient in your thinking and quick on your feet when choosing to invest in this manner.

BRRRR Method

Pros

With this method, there are numerous advantages that make investing in this way very attractive to many investors. One of the biggest draws is simply that you have access to leverage, allowing you to withdraw a significant portion of your initial investment to invest in another property. This way, you are using your current investment to fund your next investment without actually using your own physical money. Additionally, this approach allows for more cash flow than many other investment opportunities, including the house-flipping method.

Another significant benefit is that you are enabling yourself to build equity through the natural appreciation and value of the property while renting it out. This is because you maintain ownership of the property for a longer period than you would with house flipping. There are also considerable tax benefits associated with owning a rental property, which can certainly be a positive aspect. Finally, there is the advantage of being able to expand and grow your real estate investment portfolio, allowing for a more diversified investment strategy that can lead to greater gains and provide some safety for your investments.

Cons

While refinancing a property does create leverage, there are also risks associated with refinancing. Nothing is ever guaranteed; a property appraisal might come in much lower than you expected, which means you may not receive as much money as you had anticipated. This could result in being tied up financially, leaving you without enough funds to invest in your next property right away. Additionally, you must consider that over-leveraging can pose a risk, especially if you are attempting to leverage your current investments recklessly by continuously borrowing without proper research or by trying to make quick money.

One definite negative aspect to consider if you choose the BRRRR method is the fact that you will be managing multiple properties simultaneously. The goal is to refinance and then have enough money to buy another rental property, repeating the process for as long as possible. This means you will have quite a few rental properties to manage, and rental properties are not a passive source of income. You will need to oversee those properties as well as manage your tenants, which could become a full-time job if you do not hire someone else to handle it.

Like any other real estate investment strategy, overall market volatility must be taken into consideration. Even if you have conducted all the necessary research, property values and rental rates are never set in stone. What you expect to gain from your property may not align with what you actually receive.

Finally, another potential drawback to consider is that the BRRRR method adds a level of complexity that exceeds many other property investment strategies. You will constantly be trying to balance buying, rehabbing, renting, and refinancing to keep this investment strategy moving forward. This is not as straightforward as it appears on paper, as there are many moving parts, and your different properties may be at various stages of the process. Balancing everything will require a significant amount of your time and energy, ensuring that you make the right decisions in each area. It is also important to note that the more properties you take on, the more complex the situation will become. Therefore, you will need to decide for yourself when it is a good time to stop and when you can purchase another property and continue the process.

SO, WHICH STRATEGY SUITS YOU BEST?

When it comes to investing in real estate, there are many different goals that people are trying to achieve. It is important to understand what your goals are so that you can make the right choices. Let's discuss some of the most popular investment goals and which type of real estate investment would be best suited for each.

Short-Term Cash Generation

If you are someone who needs a quick turnaround time to get your money out of your investment as soon as possible, then house flipping is a better option. With house flipping, you can expect to see returns within a few months, and it offers a very clear path toward achieving your short-term returns.

Long-Term Wealth Building

If your goal is to build wealth gradually over a longer period, then the BRRRR method of real estate investing is a better choice. You are essentially building equity over the years, even if you don't have physical cash in hand. Eventually, your properties will appreciate in value, and you will also be able to purchase many more properties through this method, thereby building your real estate investment portfolio. This approach works well for people who do not need quick cash or who have longer-term financial goals.

People with Limited Capital

If you are someone who is starting off with limited capital, you can definitely get involved in both house flipping and BRRRR. However, house flipping is a bit riskier, and in many cases, you will need a large amount of money available to purchase the property and renovate it quickly. While you can take out loans for this, you must handle your finances very well to ensure that you don't go into debt or overextend yourself.

With the BRRRR method, you can get involved with a lower amount of capital on hand. This is because you are refinancing your properties and pulling out a majority of your original investment so that you can reinvest it. Essentially, you are using the same money to continue investing without having to invest more than the original amount. Just bear in mind that whichever form of real estate investing you are trying to pursue, some capital will be needed to get started, and real estate investing is a type of investment that requires significantly more upfront than many other types of investing.

Passive vs. Active Investors

Some investors prefer to be more hands-on and active in their investments, while others favor a more passive approach. Neither is right nor wrong, but it is important to understand what you are getting into and what you can handle. In general, house flipping is a more hands-on type of investment. During the time you are renovating the property, you'll need to oversee the entire process to ensure that everything is going well. You are also responsible for managing the finances and the contractors. Additionally, you must get involved with marketing and selling the property.

Many people don't realize how much work this entails because they hope to simply give directions to the contractors and then only get involved at the end when it's time to sell. However, this is not realistic. If you do not have the time or the capacity to be hands-on with the property, then house flipping might not be the best choice for you.

The BRRRR method is hands-on at the beginning, but once everything has stabilized, it becomes a more passive form of income. Once you have your properties and have found tenants, you don't really have to do much because you become a landlord, and you only need to get involved if there is a problem. The only other time you will have to be very hands-on is when you purchase another property and need to renovate it in order to rent it out again. You are in control of how many properties you have, so if you do not have the capacity to renovate and reestablish a property, then you can simply manage the ones that you currently have, and they will still bring you an income, even if you're not doing much.

EVALUATING SUITABILITY BASED ON PERSONAL FACTORS

Every investor is different, and that means it is essential to evaluate how suitable an investment style is based on your personal factors. Many different elements come into play when considering an investment style, and asking the right questions will yield the best results. Remember that there are no right or wrong answers, but it is important to be completely honest with yourself so that you can identify which investment style will be best for you.

Time Frame Considerations

When it comes to the timeframe in which you can access your investment funds, each of these investment methods offers something different. BRRRR is more about creating long-term wealth, which means you don't always have immediate access to your funds, whereas house flipping provides much quicker returns. If you are trying to determine which option is best for you, consider asking yourself some of the following questions:

- How soon do I need to see results and financial returns from my investments?
- Am I looking for something that will provide a quick profit, or do I want to build something that will last for a long time?
- Can I commit to the hands-on renovation process for the next couple of months, or do I prefer something more steady over time?

Cash Flow vs. Lump Sum

With house flipping, you can expect to receive a lump sum of money once you sell your property for a profit. You will not receive any additional money from this investment after it has been sold. In contrast, with the BRRRR method, you can anticipate smaller returns on investment over a longer period because you will be earning rental income while renting out the property. Here are some questions you can ask yourself to determine whether you prefer long-term cash flow or a short-term lump sum:

- Do I need a one-time payout, or am I more comfortable receiving small amounts of money consistently each month?

- Would I be disciplined enough to manage my finances properly if I received a lump sum from a house flip?
- Is it better for me to have an automatic monthly income that can help supplement my day job or cover some of my regular expenses?

Tax Implications

Whenever we talk about money, one aspect that always needs to be considered is the tax implications. When you are considering house flipping, you must understand that the profits you earn will be taxed as ordinary income. However, with the BRRRR method, you benefit from aspects such as depreciation and other tax deductions. With rental properties, you receive tax deductions that arise from homeownership as well as deductions that are specific to rentals. Here are the questions to ask yourself:

- Am I fully aware of the tax implications that come with receiving a large profit from a house flip?
- Do I believe that there are benefits to tax rates, depreciation, mortgage interest, and other tax advantages associated with rentals?
- Do I fully understand property tax in my state and what the implications are for both of these investment methods?

Risk Assessment

Any kind of investment comes with a certain level of risk; however, some investments are riskier than others. Additionally, you must consider the types of risks you will incur with each method. For example, when it comes to house flipping, you need to account for the risks of market fluctuations as well as unexpected renovation surprises. Not everything is clear-cut with this type of investment, and while you might plan to sell your property for a specific amount, this may not reflect the reality of the situation when you put the house on the market. Sometimes, the housing market takes a dive, and properties are simply selling for much less than you might have predicted. The risk of unexpected renovation costs is another significant concern, and anyone who has renovated a property will tell you that there are far more surprises than you might anticipate. You only fully understand the extent of the damage or the renovation costs while you are in the thick of it.

There are also definite risks associated with renting out a property. For example, you must be aware that tenant management comes with its own challenges. You might encounter a difficult tenant who makes your life incredibly challenging or one who simply does not pay their rent on time. This has implications for your financial planning, and it can be quite difficult to evict someone, depending on the laws in your country or state. Another risk associated with the BRRRR method is refinancing risks. In some cases, the process is not as straightforward as applying for refinancing and then simply getting approved. Nothing is set in stone until you have signed all of the papers.

With all of these risks in mind, here are some questions that can help you assess which kinds you can tolerate and which ones are simply not worth it for you:

- Am I capable of handling risks such as a delayed permit, a burst pipe, or a property that cannot be sold quickly?
- Do I prefer the risks associated with tenant issues or refinancing, or the risks related to market timing and renovation?
- If things do not go according to plan, which would stress me out the most: sitting on a property that is not selling or

dealing with a rental property that is vacant for an extended period?

Personality Fit

Another important aspect to consider is your personality. Each one of us is unique, and that means we all have our own personalities, which come with particular strengths, weaknesses, and preferences. Some people are more tolerant of risk, while others are more patient, and we also have individuals who might be a bit more cautious. Here are some questions that you can ask yourself to understand how your personality fits into the type of investment strategy you are considering:

- Do I like the idea of managing a property, making quick decisions, and being hands-on, or do I prefer something more stable and a slow burn when it comes to my investments?
- Does the idea of dealing with tenants and managing a property excite me or drain me?
- Do I prefer a predictable income that might take longer to establish, or am I able to handle short-term stress for a bigger short-term payoff?

In this chapter, we covered the differences between house flipping and the BRRRR method in real estate investing. It is crucial to understand both before you commit to a property investment. Regardless of which investment method you choose, one of the biggest challenges that beginners face is limited funds. In the next chapter, we will dive into practical methods to begin real estate investing without having substantial capital at your fingertips.

HOW TO GET STARTED WITHOUT A LOT OF MONEY

According to a 2023 report by the National Association of Realtors, only 26% of home buyers paid cash for their homes, while 74% relied on financing options (2024).

FINANCING OPTIONS THAT DON'T REQUIRE HUGE SAVINGS

Financing is undoubtedly a significant consideration when it comes to real estate investing. Most people simply do not have the capital to invest in cash and will need to explore various financing options to make their real estate dreams come true. The very idea of financing a property can deter people from investing because it seems like a tedious and difficult process. However, this is not necessarily the case, as there are financing options that offer flexibility and are more beginner-friendly.

FHA Loan

One option could be a Federal Housing Administration (FHA) loan, which is a loan insured by the government. With this type of loan, you are required to provide a lower down payment than with other, more traditional loans from a financial service provider or a bank. It is also more accessible for beginners because you might not need as high a credit score to be approved for this type of loan. These loans were designed to help people in lower-income brackets purchase property.

Even though the requirements for an FHA loan are lower than those for other types of property loans, there are still some criteria that must be met to obtain one. For example, you will need to have a credit score of at least 580 to qualify. A down payment is also required for this loan, but it can be as low as 3.5% (Segal 2025). Compared to the much higher down payment percentages required for other loans, this is significantly more accessible for people who do not have substantial finances or cash on hand. If you have a credit score lower than 580, you can still access this loan, but it will require a higher down payment. As you can see, there is a lot of flexibility with an FHA loan, making it more accessible to many people.

There are also some basic qualifications you need to meet to be considered for this type of loan. Some of these requirements include having a Social Security number, legally residing in the US, being of legal age, having a qualifying credit score, providing proof of employment, and demonstrating sufficient income to handle the loan. As with any other loan process, there are no guarantees that you will receive the loan. You will need to apply and go through the process, and once you are approved, you will have access to the funds.

One important aspect of this type of loan is the fact that the property needs to be your principal residence. This means that you cannot use this loan to finance property that you do not live in. This does put some restrictions in terms of investment potential, as you won't be able to use this loan to purchase a property to flip or to purchase a property immediately to rent out.

However, a detached or semi-detached house, townhouse, condominium, or anything similar can be FHA approved, and you can rent out a part of your residence. Typically, this method is called house hacking, where you live within a part of the property and rent out another part of it. Essentially, you are using the rent that you are getting from part of your property to pay off your entire mortgage, so you are living in the property for free.

VA Loan

This is a type of loan that is available through the US Department of Veterans Affairs. It helps active service members and their spouses become homeowners. This type of loan can be used to either purchase a property or build, improve, and repair one. It can also be used to refinance an existing mortgage. This type of loan has significant benefits over other types of loans if you are a veteran. There is no down payment required, and sometimes there is no private mortgage insurance required. Even though this is a type of loan that sounds very appealing to most people, there are only a few people who will qualify for it based on their veteran status. If you are a veteran or the spouse of a veteran, then you can consider this as an avenue for you.

Hard Money Lenders

A hard money loan works very differently from other types of loans you obtain from a bank or financial service provider. This type of loan is issued by an individual or a private company to help someone purchase a property. A hard money loan is backed by the property rather than the creditworthiness of the person taking out the loan. When you take out a traditional loan, you must prove that you will be able to pay it back with interest; however, with a hard money loan, you are putting up the property as collateral. If you are unable to repay the loan, the lenders can take the property from you and sell it to recover their money.

Since a hard money loan is backed by collateral rather than your credit score or borrowing history, it is much easier to obtain this type of loan. However, it is important to be aware that with this type of loan, you will be paying significantly more interest. The interest rate is set by the person or entity loaning you the money and can range anywhere from 10% to 18%. This can be risky if you plan to pay off the loan over a long period. If you are taking out a loan to flip a house, this could be a good option because you will be repaying the loan relatively quickly, so the interest won't have as much of an effect.

Private Lenders

A private lender is an individual or a company that offers a loan outside of a traditional mortgage loan. The entity or individual will fund the loan from their own resources. Since it is private, the person or entity loaning you the money will set the terms and conditions, which can vary greatly depending on who you are obtaining the loan from.

Even though these types of loans are privately managed, there are still some criteria that you need to meet in order to access them. Just bear in mind that this is definitely not set in stone, and you will have to talk with the lender to properly define their requirements. Typically, a down payment of around 20% or more is expected, as well as having the property professionally appraised for its value. You will also need a good credit score, which should be above 620, along with proof of income to demonstrate to the lender that you have the necessary funds to repay the loan (Martin 2025).

ALTERNATIVE ENTRY POINTS THAT DON'T REQUIRE BUYING RIGHT AWAY

In some cases, you might not want to purchase a property outright. There are some excellent options to still be able to have a property and make money from it without following the traditional methods.

House Hacking

House hacking is becoming increasingly popular for those looking to invest in real estate. We have already briefly mentioned what it is, but let's do a quick recap. House hacking is when you generate income from your home and then use that income to pay off your mortgage, allowing you to stay in the property for free. This can be done by dividing your property and living in one section while renting out the other for income. It is typically easier to house hack if you purchase a multifamily property, as it is simpler to divide it into different sections.

There are other ways to house hack without having a multifamily home; you just have to be a little more creative. For example, you could find a roommate to share your space with. You could also rent out your garage, yard space, or extra room as storage for people to keep their belongings. If you live in a densely populated area where parking is hard to come by, you could rent out a parking space. All of these options are great for house hacking, and you can even implement more than one, depending on the size and layout of your property.

Partnership

Another avenue you could explore is a real estate partnership. This is where you combine the strengths of two people to split the work and make things easier for both parties. In a partnership, there is typically a financial component as well as a time and effort component. One person might have the funds, while the other might have the expertise, time, and resources to manage the property and handle all of the real estate affairs. You can think of this as an active participant and a passive participant. These two different strengths, when combined, can lead to a lucrative investment opportunity for everyone involved.

When entering into a partnership with someone else, it is crucial to hash out all the details and draw up a contract so that everyone knows their responsibilities. Doing this at the beginning means that nobody will overstep their boundaries, which will cause much less friction down the line.

You could have a real estate limited partnership or a general partnership that falls under this category. In a real estate limited partnership, there is a general partner and a limited partner. The limited partner is the one who funds the investment, while the general partner takes care of the day-to-day operations regarding the investment. If you enter into a general partnership, it means that there is more than one person who will be a general owner and will be responsible for the day-to-day management and decisions regarding the investment. In this case, each partner will have equal rights and responsibilities in decision-making and all other matters concerning the property.

Wholesaling

Real estate wholesaling is an interesting approach to real estate investment. With this strategy, you purchase a property and then almost immediately sell it for a profit. You won't need to make any significant improvements or changes to the property; essentially, you are just acting as the middleman. For the strategy to work, you will need to be on the lookout for great deals when properties go on sale. You are looking to purchase a property that is sold below its market value so that you can make a profit when you resell it.

The turnaround time for property wholesaling should be quite quick to limit risks and enable you to receive your profit as soon as possible. This is typically done with distressed properties and individuals who are looking to sell their properties quickly. Once you find a property, you'll need to contact the seller and discuss how a wholesale real estate transaction works. You will then need to obtain a property contract, which must include the right to assign the contract to another party. You are not purchasing the property; rather, you are the person who will find someone to buy it. You will need to agree on how much the seller wants to make from the property so that you can keep the remainder as your profit.

Once all of this is in place, you will need to find a cash buyer. This is important because the seller will want the money as quickly as possible, and you will want your profit as well. Once everything is finalized, all you need to do is reassign the contract to the buyer and close the deal.

REAL EXAMPLES OF LOW-BUDGET DEALS

Jackson is someone who has a lot of experience in real estate and wants to use a hard money loan to help him make another real estate investment. As he was doing his research, he came across a distressed property that was in a really good neighborhood. He could see the potential in this property; all it needed was a little bit of love and some hard work. He knew that if he didn't make a move on this property, it was likely to be sold quite quickly, given that it was cheap and in a good area. He decided to take out a hard money loan since this was going to be the easiest and fastest option for him to obtain financing for the property.

Once he had access to the funds, he purchased the property, and it was time to get to work. He started renovating and updating the property to make it more modern and usable. Since it was an older property, it was very sturdy and well-made, so there weren't any huge structural changes that he had to make. He made sure to choose renovations that would provide a maximum return on his investment. He also ensured that he selected contractors he trusted and who were reputable in the real estate market. He didn't have the time or the money to waste on redoing something due to a botched job by an unreliable contractor.

The entire renovation process took about three months, and at this point, it was time to put the property on the market. Since the quality of work was high and the property looked great in a good area, it sold pretty quickly and at the price he was aiming for. He made a great return on investment through the profit he gained from the property. He was also able to pay off his hard money loan very quickly, so the high interest rate did not impact him significantly. This built his confidence in house flipping and real estate investing, so he continued doing it and made sure to conduct thorough research to make the process smoother and maximize his profit.

SIMPLE FIRST STEPS

Working toward your first real estate deal is an incredibly exciting process, but there are also steps you need to take to ensure that you are doing it properly. Let's take a look at these.

Check Your Credit Score

The first thing you'll need to do is check your credit score. Having a good credit score will significantly open up your options for obtaining a loan and financing your real estate investment. They say knowledge is power, so knowing your credit score is essential. This will help you determine whether you need to work on improving your score, and then you can create a plan to do this effectively over the next few months and years.

It is relatively easy to check your credit score. All you need to do is enter your information on your credit bureau's website, and it should pull up your credit information. You should actually check your credit score fairly often to ensure that there aren't any errors in your credit report and to confirm that you are moving in a positive direction.

Research Local Loan Programs

Every state has different loan programs, so it is important to understand which ones will be available to you before you even begin trying to finance a property. Simply conducting some internet research will help you discover what programs are available and what you need to do to qualify for them. If you don't qualify for a loan right now, you can create a plan to build yourself up to the point where you do qualify for one.

Make a List of Local Investor Meetups or Groups

Sharing ideas and knowledge with other investors is crucial. This is why getting together with other real estate investors is so important. You will gain insights and knowledge that you can't obtain anywhere else, plus other investors will be able to provide you with accurate advice based on their real experiences. They might also be able to assist you on your real estate journey, so making these connections is highly important.

You can look at social media or conduct an internet search to find your local investor meetups and groups. It might seem daunting to try joining one of these associations, but you'll find that people are much more helpful and friendly than you might think. Building your network is one of the most important things anyone can do in their professional life. We all need a helping hand sometimes, and having people who are in the same field as you is a great way to receive the right assistance and advice.

Talking to a Local Real Estate Agent or Mortgage Broker

When you are dealing with real estate, you will need to contact a real estate agent or a mortgage broker at some point. Doing this as early as possible is a great idea. Real estate agents possess extensive knowledge of the local real estate market, and they can help you understand the market you are trying to enter and what you need to do to be successful. They can offer guidance and tips on how to search for the right property, and they can assist you throughout the entire real estate process. A mortgage broker is an expert in the mortgage process, and they can help you understand what you need to do to qualify for a mortgage with a favorable interest rate. Building relationships with these types of professionals will aid you in your real estate investment journey and ensure that you are not scrambling to find these experts when you are ready to start investing or buying.

Investing can often seem very complicated and expensive, but there are many low-barrier ways to begin investing. Whether it's choosing nontraditional financing options or using an entry strategy like house hacking, you can definitely enter the real estate market with confidence as a beginner. Your first step does not have to be significant; it just needs to be intentional.

Hopefully, you now have the confidence to embark on your real estate journey. In the next chapter, we will shift gears so that you can learn how to find good deals and evaluate potential properties, setting yourself up for success. It is possible to start your real estate journey without a large down payment or the perfect financial situation. However, you do need to know how to identify the right property, and that will be our focus in the next chapter. The goal is to find undervalued properties, which will work for both house flipping and the BRRRR method.

PART II

TAKE ACTION AND MAKE SMART MOVES

3

FINDING THE RIGHT PROPERTIES

I n 2024, approximately 10% of real estate transactions were off-market deals, highlighting the growing importance of alternative sourcing methods in a competitive market (Dodge 2025).

EXPLORING PROPERTY SOURCING METHODS

Having a solid plan to secure financing for your real estate investment is the first step. Now that that's out of the way, we can focus on how to find potential investment properties. Just because you can afford a property or it looks good on the outside, doesn't mean it will make a great investment. Therefore, it is important to understand what you are doing when searching for a real estate investment property.

Multiple Listing Service (MLS)

A multiple listing service is a database that a real estate agent creates based on the information they have for a particular area. This is a handy tool for real estate agents because it allows other agents to see the MLS and connect buyers to various listings. Someone looking to purchase a property can also consult an MLS to find information about properties that are on the market and then make comparisons. Typically, this kind of database is electronic and online, making it easily updated and accessible for everyone. You can contact your local real estate agent and ask for their MLS if you cannot easily find it online. You will need to partner with a real estate agent in the area to gain access to some of these databases.

There is a wealth of information available on an MLS that can help you make better decisions when searching for a potential property. The information in each database will depend on the real estate agent who set it up. However, some information you can expect to see includes sales data, the structural components of the property, the interior features, and any special attributes.

Off-Market Deals

Most properties that are up for sale can be found on a multiple listing service, but there are also other ways to find a property. These are known as off-market homes, and they might provide you with the opportunity to access a better deal through a private avenue. They are more exclusive than the properties listed on an MLS, and only a single real estate agent will handle the buying and selling of them.

The reason a real estate agent might want to keep this information to themselves is that it results in less competition in the real estate market. It is also better for flexible negotiation since buyers and sellers can speak directly with one another to come up with a deal that works best for everyone. Additionally, there won't be the added pressure of traditional real estate sales timelines or the stress of having multiple people making offers on the property at the same time.

Finding an off-market listing can be a bit more difficult. Your best bet is to contact your local real estate agent and ask them directly if they have any off-market homes currently available. Another avenue to explore is online property websites. You might need to survey quite a few properties to find what you're looking for. However, if there are filters, see if you can filter by unlisted or for-sale-by-owner options.

Another important tool when looking for off-market properties is networking and approaching homeowners directly. If you have a network, see if you can put out feelers to indicate that you are interested in purchasing an off-market property, and then simply wait to see who responds. Your network is a very powerful tool because you never know who can assist you in your real estate investment journey. Building a network is something you will continuously do as you meet more people. This will be an ongoing part of your real estate journey, so working on your networking skills is key.

APPLYING INVESTMENT RULES

There are a few very helpful investment rules that you can use when investing in real estate. The rules you will be using will also depend on the type of real estate investment you are pursuing and what you plan to do with your property.

70% Rule for Flipping

The 70% rule is a great guideline for flipping a house. Essentially, when you take on a house-flipping project, the goal is to purchase your property for as low a price as possible so that you can reap a much larger profit when you sell. If you spend too much money on buying the house and on renovations, you will struggle to achieve any reasonable profit when you sell the house. This is why it is important to know what the home's sale price will be before you start making any purchases. This is where the 70% rule comes in to help you.

With the 70% rule, you should not pay more than 70% of your property's after-repair value, subtracting the cost of the repairs and renovations you will be making to the property. The after-repair value is simply the amount that the property could possibly sell for after you have fixed it up. To use this rule, you will need to estimate how much you think the property will sell for, multiply that by 70%, and then subtract your estimated renovation costs.

From here, you will arrive at the maximum amount you can pay for a property while still achieving a good profit. Just remember that this rule is simply a guideline to help you determine how much a property is worth or how much you should be paying for it. It is not a hard and fast rule that you must abide by. Other factors may come into play that could sway your decision or change the amount you need to pay for a property.

Also, remember that this method relies on many estimations, which means there are limitations to its accuracy. This is why it is crucial to spend some time researching the market and ensuring that you understand its ups and downs. This will also provide you with an indicator of what you can expect from the market and help you make better decisions going forward.

1% Rule for Rentals

The 1% rule is a useful guideline that you can apply with the BRRRR method or any other real estate investing strategy where you plan to rent out a property. With this rule, you simply multiply the purchase price of the property, including any necessary repairs, by 1%. The resulting figure will represent the amount of monthly rent you can set as your baseline when renting out the property. Although this is not a hard and fast rule, it provides a good estimate of your potential monthly cash flow when renting out your property.

It offers a starting point, but it is advisable to consider other factors, such as the general market rate in your area. You may have acquired a property at a bargain price and are paying a very low amount for a property in a desirable location. In this case, you might be able to charge more for rent than what the 1% rule suggests. You would use the 1% rule as your baseline and then take additional factors into account to maximize your rental profit.

UTILIZING ANALYTICAL TOOLS

These days, there are numerous tools at your disposal. You can leverage these to your advantage and simplify your real estate journey.

After-Repair Value (ARV) Calculators

The formula to calculate the after-repair value is straightforward: After-Repair Value = Purchase Price + Renovation Cost. However, you do not need to do the math yourself, as there are online calculators that perform all the calculations for you. These tools are user-friendly and accurate because they also consider other factors, such as the location of your property. One of these calculators can be found here: https://tools.reikit.com/comps/.

Return on Investment (ROI) Calculators

The goal of an investment is to make you money, so knowing the return on investment (ROI) is vital. This knowledge will help you predict how much you will gain from your investment. You can use this information to decide whether this is a good investment. The ROI is expressed as a percentage; therefore, the higher the percentage, the better the investment. There are two methods that can be used to calculate ROI: the cost method and the out-of-pocket method.

The basic formula for calculating ROI is as follows:

ROI = (Investment Gain – Investment Cost) / Investment Cost

Let's discuss the cost method first. With this method, you take into consideration the total cost of the investment. This encompasses the price you paid to buy the property and the cost of any renovations or improvements made. For example, if you bought a property for $100,000, spent $20,000 fixing it up, and then sold it for $160,000, you would calculate it as follows:

(160,000 – 120,000) / 120,000 = 33%

The out-of-pocket method is based on your invested money. It factors in the use of borrowed or leveraged money, so you would typically see a higher number when calculating the ROI. Let's use similar numbers as above. The purchase price of the property is $100,000, with a down payment of $30,000. The renovations cost you $20,000, which makes your out-of-pocket expenses $50,000. You sold the property for $160,000. Now, use these numbers to calculate ROI:

(160,000 – 120,000) / 50,000 = 80%

A good ROI calculator can be found here: https://www.calculator. net/roi-calculator.html.

Deal Analysis Software

There is a lot that goes into analyzing a deal, but you do not have to do everything yourself because there are platforms that do most of it for you. The ones I recommended you check out are:

- DealCheck: https://dealcheck.io/
- DealMachine: https://www.dealmachine.com/
- PropStream: https://www.propstream.com/
- Mashvisor: https://www.mashvisor.com/

SELECTING THE RIGHT MARKET AND
NEIGHBORHOOD

It is crucial to choose the right neighborhood when investing in real estate. This decision can make or break your investment, so it is essential to conduct thorough research when selecting the neighborhood. A real estate market analysis is also known as a comparative market analysis. This is where you analyze the current market values of properties and compare them to the property you are considering buying or selling. This is one of the best and easiest ways to conduct a real estate market analysis.

When performing this type of comparative market analysis, the goal is to help you decide whether or not you should invest in a specific area. This is especially helpful if you are wondering about purchasing a property in two or three different cities. You can compare and determine which option is better. This type of market analysis also helps you identify elements that could potentially hinder the success of your investment in certain areas. Additionally, you will gain insight into the demographics of the area, allowing you to fully understand the future potential of the neighborhood. All of these factors are essential for understanding your potential investment. Let's delve into more detail about the steps you will need to follow to conduct a market analysis.

Step 1: Be Informed About the Market

The first step is always to be informed about the market. You need to understand the market you are working with in order to make the best decisions regarding it. In this initial step, you should look at things from a global or broad perspective without delving deeply into the specifics or details. This broad perspective is necessary to form the foundation of your analysis and ensure that you understand the situation from a larger viewpoint.

The real estate market is always evolving and changing, so it's important to stay on top of what is happening, as well as observe the trends. Take a look at what the real estate market looks like now and how it is performing. You can gain valuable insights into what the market might look like by examining economic indicators; if the economy is doing well, it will likely be reflected in the real estate market as well.

It is also a good idea to analyze your competitors to see what they are offering or doing so that you can gain a better understanding for yourself. If they are being more aggressive with their investment strategies, try to understand why this is the case, and then see if you can apply a similar strategy to your investments. It is not advisable to simply copy someone else's investment strategy or analysis of the market, so make sure that you conduct your own research and support what you observe with your competitors using your knowledge and expertise.

Step 2: Know the Customers in the Market

Knowing your customers is vital when you are trying to understand a market or when you are investing in real estate in general. This can also be referred to as understanding the current demand in the market. Who is looking for what kind of property? How many people are searching for property? What is attracting potential customers to certain properties? These are all great questions to start asking yourself so that you can fully understand the potential customers in the market.

A good starting point is to ask yourself how many customers are currently in the real estate market and how this is changing over time. A market analysis is not something you will conduct at one static point; rather, it is something you will continuously perform to track changes to understand how things are evolving. See if you can identify whether the demand is increasing, decreasing, or remaining the same. You will also need to know who your real estate customers are and where they are located. Examine their consumption rates and behaviors. It might also be beneficial to understand what the budget of your customers is, as well as the common factors that tend to trigger a purchase.

Step 3: Study in Detail What Your Competitors Already Offer

You might not be too excited about having many competitors, but you can use your competition to your advantage. When you have direct competition, it means that you and a few others are all competing for the same customers or potential investment opportunities. This indicates that your competitors have been researching matters pertaining to you and your investments as well. Consequently, you can obtain vital information by studying their behavior and gaining a deeper understanding of it.

The first thing you will need to do is figure out who your competitors in the market are. They could be individual investors or even larger companies. Try to determine their investment strategies and whether or not they have been successful over the long term. Examine their trends as well as any public financial data you can find. All of this will help you understand your competitors more deeply, and it will also assist you in grasping the market in which they operate. If someone else has made a mistake that did not work out, you can learn from their errors rather than repeating the same ones yourself. This will help you achieve greater success in a shorter period of time, so it is definitely something you should not overlook.

Step 4: Analyze the Factors That May Influence the Market

There are many factors that could potentially influence the market that may not be directly related to actual real estate. For example, there may have been technological developments, or new laws and regulations might have been enacted. There may also be a new real estate trend that emerges, making certain properties more attractive than others.

Step 5: Collect Data to Determine If the Project Is Viable and Secure

Data collection is an underrated but very important part of real estate market research. When you collect data, you are essentially gathering information that will assist you in determining whether a project is a good investment or if it is something you need to move on from. Some of the data you will need to collect includes demographic and socioeconomic information. This is important because it will help you understand the demand for the property and what is happening in the area. For example, if there is an area experiencing a large influx of younger families, this indicates that it is an affordable area, and the demand for housing will likely increase over the next few years.

You can use various tools to help you collect and analyze the data for the property or area in which you are looking to invest. Some of the most helpful tools include property management software, such as a real estate CRM system, which helps you manage your real estate portfolio. You can also examine heat maps, which will show you where there is high demand for properties and where there is potential for growth. You might even want to conduct property surveys in the area to gain a more hands-on understanding of what is happening locally.

Evaluate a Neighborhood Before Investing

When it comes to investing in property, it can be more important to invest in a good area than to focus solely on a specific property. When you consider purchasing a property, you will likely choose an area first and then look for properties within that area to see if anything meets your needs and standards. Typically, it does not work the other way around, where you would search for a specific property and then evaluate the area to see if it suits your requirements. A specific neighborhood or area will have benefits and amenities that align with the lifestyles of certain individuals, which is why selecting the right neighborhood is so crucial for investors.

Regardless of who your target customer or tenant is, it is important to consider the amenities that are close to your potential property investment. The more amenities that are nearby, the better your chances of attracting the right kinds of tenants. It is true that different demographics will desire different amenities. For example, a young single person who is just starting out in their career might want to be closer to city life, with social meetup spots like restaurants and bars nearby, whereas families are looking for proximity to good schools, parks, and family-friendly facilities. In general, you would like the neighborhood you are investing in to have good schools, restaurants, shops, gyms, medical facilities, and recreational activities close by.

Another key indicator of a good area is its proximity to employment. Many people choose to live close to where they work, so if there are many job opportunities in an area, it will be attractive to a lot more people. This doesn't necessarily mean that it has to be in the economic hub, but being near an area with more job availability is advantageous. You should also consider factors like crime rates, as everyone would prefer to live in a place with a lower crime rate.

If you want to get a good idea of what is happening in a specific neighborhood or area, it is advisable to get in your car and drive around or walk through the neighborhood. You will see what is actually going on, apart from what you can research. If you notice a lot of rundown properties where it appears that the residents do not take pride in their homes, this is not a good sign. It is also a red flag if you see many signs indicating "for rent" or "for sale." You don't want a large number of vacant properties in an area, as this indicates that people do not want to live there and that more people are moving out than moving in. The only exception would be a neighborhood or area with a lot of new development and new builds, as this will naturally have more properties for sale or rent.

Even though it can seem like a tedious job, doing your research on the neighborhood and the properties you want to invest in is a key part of the real estate investment journey. It is going to save you a lot of time, money, and resources in the long run, and you'll be thankful that you spent a little extra effort doing the groundwork before putting down your money for an investment. The great thing is that there are many tools available that can really help you ensure you have the best chance at a successful investment, so it is a good idea to use these to your advantage. The goal is to be able to make the most informed decisions you can as you embark on your real estate investment journey.

Now that you can identify promising properties, your next step is to understand how to effectively rehabilitate a property to maximize its value and your potential returns. In the next chapter, we will dive into the renovation process so that you can understand key elements such as budgeting, planning, and executing successful property rehabilitation.

REHAB WITHOUT REGRET

I n 2024, Americans spent an estimated $603 billion on home remodeling, with 46% of home buyers being less willing to compromise on the condition of the home when purchasing (National Association of Realtors 2025). This highlights the importance of well-executed renovations in the real estate market.

THE REHAB PROCESS

There is a lot that goes into the rehab process when it comes to real estate. Knowing the full extent of what is expected is fundamental to ensuring your success. Let's discuss some of the things you will need to consider as you embark on this journey.

The first thing you need to do is plan and work out your design for your property. Many people like to skip this step because it seems like a waste of time, and they believe it will take too long. If you are the type of person who just likes to dive into something, then the planning and preparation phase is probably the part you will dislike the most. However, it is one of the most important things you can do to ensure a smooth process from start to finish.

Think about building a house from scratch; you will want to make sure that the foundation is set and solid before you start with anything else. If you do not have a solid and secure foundation, as you continue building your house, there is a risk that the foundation will give way, ruining all the hard work you have put in throughout the rest of the process. Then, you will need to break down everything you have done and start from the bottom again. I'm sure this is not something you want to do, which is why it is important to recognize that planning and preparation are the foundation of everything else that comes afterward.

If you are undertaking a larger renovation, you will also need to consider the time and resources required for the demolition. You might want to remove a certain part of the property to create space for something else, or it may simply be an eyesore that you wish to eliminate. Following that, the rebuilding phase will commence, during which you will begin to see tangible progress toward making the space look the way you envision. In some cases, the rebuilding phase may not take too long; however, if you are making significant changes to the property, you should plan for it to be quite resource-intensive and time-consuming. Additionally, you will need to consider the installation of essential systems such as plumbing, HVAC, electrical, and mechanical components. All of this is crucial to ensure that your property and home function at their best and meet all safety standards.

Once you have the structure and these important elements in place, you can move on to your walls and flooring. It may be the case that you do not need to break down or build up much, so you would only need to redo the flooring or certain walls. Other tasks you might need to undertake include adding cabinets, appliances, and final touches. This is definitely the more enjoyable part of the process, as you can see your vision coming to life; however, it requires careful planning and time to get it right. Along the way, you may discover that some of your initial plans do not work out as expected, necessitating adjustments. This is a very normal part of the process, and it is something you should anticipate. Let's discuss in more depth the steps you will take as you navigate the rehabilitation process.

Step 1: Make a Plan

As mentioned above, it is crucial to start your process by making a solid plan. This is where you establish your priorities so you know exactly what you will be working on first and how you will proceed through the process. It also helps you stay on track and ensures that you do not get caught up in details that are not important.

Step 2: Set a Budget

Part of the planning process is budgeting, which is essential. It is easy to go off course and spend significantly more money than you have available. When you budget, you can allocate your funds to the most important items and ensure that you will not run out at crucial moments. When budgeting, make sure to keep about 10% to 20% of the total amount for unforeseen circumstances and expenses. As much as planning is essential, unexpected bumps in the road can arise, and it is important to have the finances to help you navigate through them.

Step 3: Hire a Contractor

Once you have set your budget, it is time to hire your contractors. If you have been through the renovation process before, you probably have one or two contractors with whom you are comfortable. If not, then it is time to start interviewing. Take your time with this, as you will be entering into a contract with this person and including them in a significant portion of the renovation process. Ensure that they have the necessary skills, certifications, and experience to help you achieve your goals. Do not choose the cheapest or most convenient option in this case.

Step 4: Talk to Your Insurance Company

You will need to ensure that you have the necessary insurance coverage, so call your insurance company before and after the renovation process is completed. Remember that when you renovate a property, it increases in value; therefore, the amount for which you were insured at the beginning of the process may not be sufficient afterward.

Step 5: Secure Permits and Order Materials

Before you start breaking ground on your renovation, it is important to ensure that you have all of the necessary permits and materials. Every county and state has different requirements regarding permits and what they allow in general. Understanding the permits you will need will help you ensure a smooth process and avoid incurring any unnecessary fines. At this stage, you should also begin securing your materials for the remainder of the building process.

Step 6: Start Demolition

Once all of this is done, you can start the demolition of the property. This is not always necessary, and it really depends on the size of your project. However, if you are undertaking significant renovations, then demolition is an important step. Even something as simple as relocating a wall requires some demolition, so keep this in mind.

Step 7: The Installs

Once the demolition is complete, you can begin rebuilding and installing the necessary and important elements. For example, you will need to finish the patching, drywall, sanding, painting, flooring, appliances, and cabinetry.

Step 8: Add the Finishing Touches

Once all that is done, it is time for you to add the finishing touches to your property. You'll want to incorporate some fixtures and hardware that will make things look appealing. This will include lighting, door handles, a backsplash, and even sealing the floor so that it looks crisp and new. You can also add other design elements, but it depends on what you are doing with the property. If you are renting out the property and choosing to do so fully furnished, then you'll need to furnish the property and ensure that it attracts the type of tenant you want. If you are planning to sell the property, then you do not need to worry about furniture or making things look pretty.

ESTIMATING COSTS AND AVOIDING SURPRISES

It can be very easy to let the cost of revamping your property skyrocket without proper planning. Expenses can quickly add up, and because you are likely to spend smaller amounts of money on many different items, it might be difficult to track. Being able to estimate your costs effectively will help you avoid any surprises down the line and ensure that you have enough money for the most important aspects of your renovation journey.

Step 1: Pick Your Projects

When you purchase a property with potential, you might have a long list of different things you want to do to increase its value. However, not all of these things will be realistic based on your timeline or budget. This is why it is so important to select the projects you want to tackle during your renovation. Since you are renovating to increase the potential profit of your property, it is best to write down a list of all the things you want to do and then prioritize them based on what would add the most value. Adding an extra bedroom or bathroom might be more beneficial than retiling the kitchen. Even though it might be nice to install new floors in the kitchen and it would increase the value, adding an extra room will be much more valuable and yield more money in the long run. It's all about planning and being smart about where you invest your money so that you can achieve the best returns while spending the least.

Step 2: Research the Costs

You will need to understand the costs associated with each of your renovation projects. There are many hidden costs that are not immediately obvious, which means that conducting thorough research will help you uncover these hidden expenses, allowing you to obtain an accurate representation of how much you will be spending. For something like retiling a floor, you will need to spend money on tiles, but that is not the only expense. You will also need cement or adhesive to adhere the tiles to the floor, as well as grout. Additionally, you might require a sealant, tools to complete the tiling job, and equipment to remove the previous flooring.

You will also need to consider the contractors or professionals you will hire to complete this job. You can consult a contractor with a specific skill set for the project you wish to undertake and ask them for an estimate of how much everything will cost, including labor. Be sure to add a little extra as a buffer in case unexpected costs arise.

Step 3: Keep a List of All Your Cost Estimates

Keeping a list will help you track all of the cost estimates you made during the planning stage. You can update this list, but it is also important to do your best to adhere to it throughout the process. This list should organize your total budget into different categories, so you know how much is allocated to each area. You can break this down into specific percentages, with the highest percentage going toward the most expensive or most important items.

Step 4: Set Your Savings Goal

Once you have estimated the costs of everything you want to do, it's time to start saving and budgeting. This is something you need to do in advance so that you have enough time to save for all the renovations you want to undertake. Depending on the type of project you are going to pursue, whether it's flipping a house or following the BRRRR framework, you might need a larger amount of money. You will be able to leverage some of the expenses through a loan so that you aren't paying the majority of the expenses out of pocket or in cash. However, it is a good idea to have some physical funds available for renovating the property. Once you know your total savings goal, you can break it down into smaller amounts to start working toward that goal.

Step 5: Collect Bids from Contractors

Now is the time to interview and collect bids from contractors. Remember what we discussed earlier: the cheapest, most convenient option might not be the best one. This is why it is so important to do your research and conduct interviews with each of your contractors. If you can obtain reviews or referrals from other people you trust who have used these contractors, that is even better, as it provides firsthand experience of how good or bad they are. You can also conduct some online research to find out if there are any online reviews, which will help you better understand your potential contractors.

Step 6: Schedule Your Renovation

Once all of this is done, your planning is almost complete, and it's time to schedule your renovation. This includes ensuring that all elements are aligned so you can start on a specific day. You will want to make sure that you have all the appropriate materials and contractors available around the same time to avoid losing precious hours due to missing materials or unavailable contractors. It helps to schedule a bit in advance to ensure that everything goes according to plan and that you have everything you need. This also gives you some time to prepare for the process ahead, which might be quite a significant task to undertake.

HIGH-ROI UPGRADES AND DIY TIPS

ROI stands for return on investment, and it refers to the amount of profit you will make after completing your investment in relation to how much money you spent. Every investor seeks to achieve a higher ROI, which means spending less money to generate more profit. Certain renovations and DIY projects yield a much higher ROI, and those are the areas you can focus on to ensure you maximize your profit. Let's discuss a few of these options, and then you can decide which ones will be best for you.

One upgrade that can bring a higher ROI is a garage door replacement. In many cases, the garage door is one of the first things people see when they enter a property. Having a modern, clean, and aesthetically pleasing garage door will significantly enhance curb appeal. Additionally, it is not very expensive, so you could potentially double your ROI with just this improvement. Continuing with the theme of curb appeal, you can replace your entry door to create a more expensive and modern look. This is something that people will notice from the outside, and they will expect something amazing on the inside as well. Plus, there is nothing better than walking through a beautifully designed doorway.

One of the most frequently used rooms in a house is the kitchen, which truly attracts potential buyers. Updating and replacing a few key elements in the kitchen can significantly increase a property's perceived value. These updates include updating countertops, replacing hardware, installing new flooring, repainting walls, and improving lighting. You can also make a few adjustments by rearranging certain amenities to enhance user-friendliness.

Everyone loves an outdoor space for enjoyment and entertaining, which is why a deck could be a great addition to your property. An outdoor deck is one of the features that truly attracts buyers to a home. The most popular types of decks are wood and composite, so you will need to choose which one best suits your needs and budget. Composite decks are more expensive, but they offer a better return on investment and are highly durable.

Another room that can significantly enhance resale value is the bathroom. There is nothing better than a modern and relaxing bathroom. When bathrooms are outdated and old-looking, they do not feel as welcoming or inviting, which can deter many potential buyers or renters from purchasing or renting a property. Adding new fixtures, tiles, lighting, and decor can greatly help modernize and improve a bathroom.

A few other aspects to consider are window replacements. This is especially relevant if the house is quite old and the windowpanes appear incredibly outdated. You can also look into replacing the floors or the roof if these elements are not up to standard or do not look as nice as they could. This depends on how much money you have to spend on renovations and should be considered last, after you have evaluated the other areas we have already discussed.

Now, remember that some tasks can definitely be done by yourself, while others require professional assistance. While it might be tempting to do everything yourself to cut costs, this can lead to bigger issues down the line. Therefore, make sure that you only undertake DIY projects that are suitable. For example, you can certainly repaint walls, replace small fixtures, change the lighting, install simple tiles, install kitchen cabinets or doors, update knobs and door handles, clean the gutters, power wash the outdoor area, and tidy up the outdoor landscape. Tasks that you should definitely hire a professional for include electrical work, plumbing, major renovations, siding, roof repairs, and structural or foundational repairs.

RECOGNIZING AND AVOIDING RED FLAGS

On this journey, there are some red flags that you should do your best to avoid in order to prevent any wasted money down the line. When looking for a potential property in which you will be investing, this is when you need to be extra alert. Certain issues can cost you significantly more money and simply won't be worth renovating, and these are the things you should avoid.

The number one item on the list is foundation problems. If a house has foundation issues, it means that you will essentially have to redo the entire house, as you will need to dismantle the existing structure before fixing the foundation. This is definitely not worth it and will require a lot of work and money. You should also look out for signs of wear and tear and an outdated design in the property. Some homes have been around for a very long time, and the general wear and tear of the structure of the property may not be what it should be. It might take considerable work and renovations to ensure that the house is modern and fully functional before you can sell or rent it out.

Another aspect to consider is safety concerns or limited function-ality with certain features of the property. You want to make sure that the property is 100% safe, and you also want to ensure that it is user-friendly. If the current layout or design of the property doesn't align with how modern people live, then it's really not going to be worth it. For example, I have seen properties where the bathrooms are outside of the main building, which seems like a nightmare for anyone living in that home on a day-to-day basis.

Significant issues like water damage, pest problems, and general environmental concerns are also things you will need to avoid if you are trying to achieve a higher ROI. The goal is to spend the least amount of money while obtaining the most returns, so when these major issues arise, it will require a lot of time, energy, and resources to resolve, making it potentially not the best choice for an investment.

Spotting Unreliable Contractors

You will need a reliable contractor throughout the process, so it's important to spot any potential red flags early on to avoid engaging further with a bad contractor. There are a few things you can consider red flags when getting a quote or thinking about moving forward with a specific contractor. One thing to be wary of is if the contractor is asking for a large down payment or if the contract is very vague. It is easy to be taken advantage of in both of these cases, so it's important for you to read through the contract and ensure it is highly specific to the job and the tasks that need to be completed. Additionally, make sure that you do not have to pay an unnecessarily large down payment that is nonrefundable should the job not be done as needed.

Another red flag to consider is if the contractor has a lot of bad reviews or no reviews at all. You want a solid track record to ensure that this person will do what they say and is good at their job. If there are no reviews or no one for you to call for references, then this is definitely something you can consider a red flag, and you should move on from this potential contractor. An estimate or bid that is extremely low is also a red flag because it could indicate that this person does not know their worth, is just starting out, or is simply trying to make a quick buck without planning to do the job properly.

You can also learn a lot from a person's communication skills. If they are not communicating effectively, missing your messages, or simply going silent for long periods, then this is not someone you want to work with on a long project. You will also need to verify your potential contractors to ensure that they have the necessary licenses; if the information does not match up, then this person is probably shady and not someone you want to work with.

Other things that can be considered red flags include asking for upfront cash payments, appearing unprofessional, or even being under the influence of alcohol or other substances. All of these behaviors are simply unprofessional, and you don't want to work with someone who will bring negative energy to your project. You want someone professional and reliable.

At the end of the day, the planning phase is likely one of the most important phases of any renovation or real estate journey. It will be extremely helpful if everything is planned properly, as this ensures that things will go much more smoothly for you moving forward. It will also help you build a proper strategy and avoid potential mishaps and mistakes because you've already planned for or anticipated them before they occur. Even though it might seem tedious, it is definitely worth it to do your research and take your time with the planning process.

Now that you have a solid understanding of the renovation process, you are ready for the next step. This will involve diving into the BRRRR strategy. In the next chapter, we will fully explore how to leverage the buy, rehab, rent, refinance, repeat method to build a scalable and profitable real estate portfolio.

5

THE BRRRR PROCESS

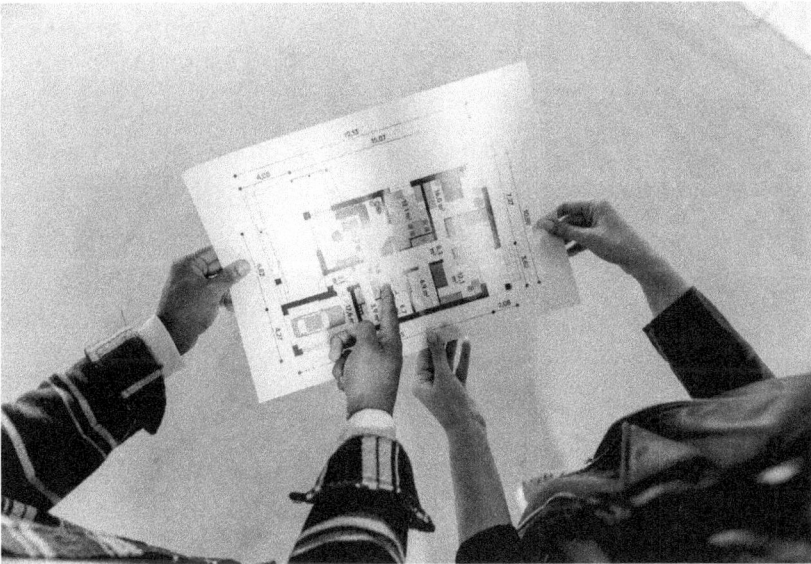

The BRRRR method is a fantastic approach to entering real estate investing due to its structured nature. Many people have found success with it, but it's important to understand the process before diving in. When you fully comprehend the process and what goes into something like this, you can make better decisions, and you can navigate this type of real estate investment much more effectively. There are numerous individuals with fantastic success stories related to this method of real estate investing, and you can be one of them.

THE BRRRR STRATEGY: A CLOSER LOOK

There are five specific steps in the BRRRR method, and each letter represents something very important. In this section, we will discuss each of these steps and explore them in greater depth so that you fully understand each one.

Buy

The first step is to buy a property. This is what the "B" stands for in BRRRR. In this initial step, you need to ensure that you are purchasing the right property to maximize your investment. This step is not only the first but also the most important. If you buy the right property, it will make all the other steps much easier and ensure that you achieve a great ROI. The goal is to purchase a property as cheaply as possible, with as few issues as possible. You should be looking for a property that is below market value. Distressed or undervalued properties can offer significant rewards after the rehabilitation process.

During this phase, you will need to conduct market research to find the right property. It will take some time, and you are unlikely to find an ideal property within the first few days. Don't get disheartened; make sure to take your time so that you don't rush into something that could cost you later on. Once you have located your ideal property, it is time to start applying for a loan to purchase it. You will also need to obtain the appropriate licensing and registration required for the potential renovations you will be undertaking.

Rehab

The second step is the rehab step. This step focuses on a lot of what we discussed in the previous chapter. It's all about renovating and rehabilitating the property so that it is ready for your potential tenant. During this step, you will also ensure that you are selecting the right contractors to work on your project.

Rent

Once your property is ready, it is time to rent it out. The goal is to secure reliable tenants who will be able to pay you your weekly or monthly rental fee so that you can make a profit. It's not only about finding the right tenant but also about setting the right rental rate to ensure a consistent cash flow. There is a lot that goes into this, but conducting some market research and evaluating how much you want to charge based on what similar properties in the area are charging is a good start. Doing this at the beginning will help you get a better idea of what you can expect once your property is up for rent.

This step also includes marketing your property to get the word out and find the right tenant. The goal should be to have as many options as possible so that you can make the best choice. Marketing could involve strategies such as online ads, newspaper ads, word-of-mouth, or even posters and billboards. It all depends on your area and what will give you the most reach.

Once the word is out and people start applying to rent your property, you will need to conduct interviews and check references to ensure that you choose the right person. You should be very wary of anyone who applies without any references. Also, make sure you perform a credit check to ensure that the person renting can afford to pay the rent.

Refinance

Once you have your tenant, it is time for the fourth step, which is refinancing. With this step, you can pull out equity from the property to use for purchasing another property and repeating the process. This step requires a lot of accounting and ensuring that your finances are in order. Throughout this process, you must manage your property well and maintain it so that your tenants are happy. You will also need to communicate effectively with your tenants and ensure that you are meeting all of the lease agreements on your end.

Repeat

The final step is to repeat, which means that you will start again with the buying process and follow the steps once more. The goal of the BRRRR method is to grow your portfolio and maximize your profit. When you repeat the strategy, it means that you will manage multiple properties simultaneously. This does require some strategy, which may mean that you need to acquire software to assist you with property management. You might also consider hiring a property manager who will take care of the day-to-day operations of your properties while you focus on building your portfolio.

RISKS BEFORE INVESTING

As with any kind of investing, there are definitely risks associated with this method. It is important to understand these risks before proceeding so that you aren't going in blind. It will also help you to develop some contingency plans should one of these risks become a reality for you.

The first and probably the biggest risk is over-leveraging. There is great potential to make a lot of money through leveraging, which is why this method is so attractive; however, over-leveraging is something you need to watch for. Over-leveraging is essentially borrowing too much money and then being unable to pay it back. You might be tempted to stretch your borrowing capacity to secure the deal you want, but when you borrow too much money, you negatively impact your cash flow, making it difficult to repay the loan.

Another point regarding over-leveraging is that if the market experiences a downturn, your property value may decline. If you have a very small buffer between the money you've leveraged and what you possess, this could lead to significant problems. It could place you in a negative equity situation, which could complicate refinancing and obtaining loans. You want to ensure that your property can stand on its own two feet, even in the event of a market downturn. It is important not to rush into the next deal quickly after renting out one of your properties. You want to ensure that the properties you currently own are secure and can operate independently before you attempt to invest further.

Another risk is underestimating the rehabilitation costs of a property. This is something we have mentioned before, and it is incredibly common. The truth is that you never truly know how much the rehabilitation will cost until you are in the thick of it. This is why it is important to do your best to estimate, but also to have a buffer amount so that if something unexpected arises, you have funds to cover it.

Along the same lines, the risk of overestimating the after-repair value is very real. This occurs when you believe that you can rent or sell your property for much more than what is actually reflected in reality. This may happen because you didn't conduct your research properly, or the market has shifted since you made your estimates. This is why it is so important to stay up-to-date with your local real estate news and to be more conservative with your estimates.

Since the BRRRR method is all about renting and finding tenants, there is a risk of getting a bad tenant who could cause more issues than benefits for you. For example, a tenant could cause property damage, lead to legal disputes, or fail to pay their rent, and all of this will be your responsibility. Another risk associated with renting is that the market may not be in your favor. It could be difficult to find a tenant, which means you will have a higher vacancy rate, and every month your property remains vacant is money lost.

Another risk involves challenges with refinancing. You may find it difficult to secure favorable refinancing terms, which means you will not be getting a good deal on your loan, and it will cost you more than you expected. Even worse, you might not be able to obtain a loan or refinance your property at all. This is why it is so important to ensure that your credit score is good and that you have established relationships with lenders so that they trust you.

KEY CONSIDERATIONS DURING REFINANCING

When refinancing your property, your aim is to secure a lower interest rate or to completely change the repayment terms of your current mortgage. This helps you save on your monthly payments, allowing you to free up more finances for other purposes. In this case, you will have more money to invest in other properties and continue growing your real estate investment portfolio.

When you refinance your mortgage, you have the opportunity to lower the interest rate you currently have, which means that over the long term, you will be paying much less for the property. You might also be able to lower the monthly premium you need to pay and obtain a shorter loan term, which all adds up to additional savings. Refinancing also allows you to change your current mortgage product to something more beneficial or better suited to you at this moment. Sometimes, we might choose an option that seems like a good idea, but as time goes on, a better option becomes available for refinancing. One of the biggest benefits of refinancing is that you can cash out some of your equity and then secure a larger loan. When you have some of your equity in cash, you can use that to reinvest in another property or area.

While there are many positive aspects to refinancing, it is also important to consider the negatives while you are trying to make this decision. There are always risks involved when it comes to investing and finances. Since refinancing is essentially like taking out a new loan, you are agreeing to new loan terms and new loan amounts, and you will likely have to pay all the closing costs again. These costs cover fees, underwriting, title deed services, and appraisal. You might expect to pay somewhere between 3% and 6% of the balance of your loan for these closing costs.

Another thing that people don't often consider is the time and research you need to do in order to select the right loan and lender. This is similar to the process you would have undertaken when you first started looking for a loan for your property investment. You likely didn't jump into the first loan or mortgage you were offered, and you would have needed to do your research to ensure you were getting the best deal. The same principle applies here, so you need to be aware that you will need to invest a lot of time and effort. It is also important to understand that your credit score might take a hit because you are taking out a new mortgage. This will likely not last very long, but be prepared for a drop in your score that could last anywhere from a few months to a couple of years. This might not be all that bad, depending on what your credit score currently is.

It is important to understand your loan-to-value (LTV) ratio so that you can know how much you owe on your current mortgage relative to the value of your property. This is an essential ratio to grasp when you are trying to refinance your property. It can significantly impact your ability to secure a favorable interest rate on your new mortgage and may also determine your eligibility for certain loans. If your LTV is on the higher side, it will be more difficult for you to obtain a loan.

Calculating this number is relatively simple; all you need to do is divide the amount you currently owe on your mortgage by the value of your property and then multiply that number by 100. You will obtain a percentage, which will represent your LTV. Depending on the type of refinancing loan you intend to pursue, you might only need a percentage of 97% or lower to qualify (Kenton, 2023). However, for certain options, such as a cash-out refinance, you will need an LTV of about 80% (Parker, 2025).

When you are going through the refinancing process, it is important to ensure that you have all your ducks in a row and that all your documentation is ready to go. You can start collecting this information as early as possible to make the process smoother when you reach the refinancing stage. You will need proof of rental income, property appraisal, and renovation receipts, to name a few of the required documents. Additionally, you can contact your preferred loan provider to inquire about any other documentation they require, ensuring that you have everything on hand to facilitate the process.

SAFELY ACCESSING EQUITY

When you are following the BRRRR method, it is important to safely access equity with as little risk to yourself as possible. We have already mentioned the cash-out refinance, which is a great way to access equity safely. With a cash-out refinance, you will use the equity in your current property to access cash, allowing you to purchase another property. This is not a second mortgage, which means it is distinct from a traditional line of credit. Essentially, you are replacing your current mortgage with a new loan that will include the balance you owe on your current property plus the equity you are borrowing to make your next investment.

All the other benefits of refinancing are still available with a cash-out refinance. For example, if there are better interest rates now than there were when you first took out your mortgage, you will benefit from lowering your overall interest rate with your new loan. This is definitely the way to go when you are following the BRRRR method, and many investors have done the same.

While leveraging can be a great tool to help you make more money through diversifying your real estate investments, there is a risk of over-leveraging. When you over-leverage, you put yourself in more debt than you can handle, or the amount of debt you have on your property exceeds its current market value. This makes it difficult to recover your funds.

The good news is that over-leveraging can be avoided. If you do your research and ensure you conduct your due diligence before purchasing a property or taking out a mortgage, you can mitigate this risk. You need to understand all the expenses that will arise from purchasing the property so that you aren't taken by surprise and require a much higher loan than expected. This means you will need to comprehend the property's expenses right from the start. Once you do that, you should also ensure that your debt-to-equity ratio is less than 70% to make sure it is manageable and that you will have good leveraging power.

It is also good practice to stick to a few investment properties rather than trying your hand at multiple investments, as these can be difficult to manage. If you are a beginner, then just stick to one or two additional properties so that you can get a feel for the BRRRR method. Once you are comfortable, you can move on to more properties. Remember that real estate investing is not a get-rich-quick scheme, which means you will likely need to take your time to ensure that you aren't losing any money.

CALCULATING CASH FLOW AND SETTING RENTS

When you are ready to start renting out your property, it is important to set the right rent so that you are not selling yourself short or making less money than you possibly could. At the end of the day, you want to maximize your profits so you can increase your cash flow. This begins with researching how much others are charging for rent for comparable properties. Look for a property that is very similar to yours and located in the same area, and see what others are charging. This will give you a good indication of how much people are willing to spend in that area for your type of property. You can easily conduct this research by visiting property websites like Zillow and even Craigslist. Remember that you will likely be able to charge more money after you have made your improvements and renovations, so you can also hire a home appraiser to help you determine the value of the property and how much you can charge in rent if you are finding it difficult to locate comparable properties.

Another factor to consider is the laws in your area, as many regions have limits on landlords regarding how much they can charge for rent. This means that the amount you charge for rent may not be entirely up to you. Rent control laws are a very real consideration depending on the city, state, or country in which you live. You'll need to ensure that you understand these laws so that you're not violating them and becoming liable for repercussions.

You will also need to check for seasonality, which means that certain seasons or times of the year will have more demand for rental properties than others. A simple example would be if you are situated in a college town; it is more likely that you will find a renter during the school term, as that is when students will flock to the town and need a place to stay. During peak times, you'll be able to charge more for rent than when demand is much lower.

A common rule that you can use when determining how much you can charge for rent is the 1% rule. It is a simple calculation where you multiply the property's value by 1%. The number you obtain will be an estimate of what you can expect to charge for rent. However, this is a very rough estimate, so it is important to take into consideration other factors such as demand, location, and market conditions. This will provide you with a starting point, and then you can conduct further research to refine the amount you will be charging for rent.

EFFECTIVE PROPERTY MANAGEMENT

When it comes to managing your property, the first thing you need to do is ensure that you find the right tenant. Finding good and reliable tenants will make things much easier for you down the road. It means that you will have someone living in your property whom you can trust, making your income more reliable and ensuring that your property is well taken care of. This is why it is so important to take your time when looking for tenants and not rush the process just to fill the vacancy.

The first step is to advertise your rental property to get the word out that you have a vacancy. This is not as simple as quickly putting up an ad on a property website and hoping for the best. You want to put your best foot forward to attract high-quality potential tenants. Firstly, you need to understand who your target market is. Look at your property and consider who your ideal tenant would be. For example, if you have a studio apartment in the middle of a big city, your tenant will likely be a couple or a single person with a career who wants to be close to the city center. You can then tailor your advertising to this specific tenant. Highlight aspects that they would find important and what they are looking for in a place to stay. If your property is a larger home with a garden and is close to good schools, your target market might be a family with small children. In this case, you should emphasize safety, amenities, children's activities, space, and other factors that parents of young children would consider important. This is what your target audience is looking for, so when they search for something, you want to be at the top of the search results.

Putting your best foot forward in advertising your property also involves taking high-quality photos. One of the biggest mistakes I see people making is that the photos they take of their properties are so poor that they deter potential applicants. Ensure that you take photos when the lighting is good, and it is also a good idea to clean up the space to make it look appealing. You might want to hire a professional to help you take stunning pictures. Once you have your photos, you will also want to create a detailed listing that highlights all the positive aspects of your property to attract your target tenant.

You don't only have to advertise on property websites because social media is also a great tool. Additionally, people you know could spread the word, and it is more likely that you will find a good-quality tenant through word-of-mouth and your network than by sifting through thousands of applications from random individuals. Speaking of your network, it is always a good idea to broaden it by speaking to local real estate agents and attending real estate investment events. This way, you can build connections with people who could possibly help you find the right tenant for your property.

Once you have a few applicants, it is time to start the tenant screening process. This is where you conduct background checks and delve deeper into who your potential tenants are so that you can make the right choice. The screening process begins with the rental application. You'll need to have your potential tenant fill out an application and provide all of their basic information to get started. This information will include their name, contact information, employer, and rental history. Your potential tenant might also want to provide additional information to help you make your decision. To ensure that you are not overwhelmed with thousands of applications from individuals who would not qualify, you can set some applicant requirements in your advertisement to immediately disqualify those you would not consider. These minimum requirements could include a certain income level or credit score.

Now that you have all of your applicants' basic information, you can run some checks to ensure that you have good candidates. These checks will include credit history, rental history, and an

250 | CHAPTER 5

overall background check. This is important because you want to
get a clear idea of how financially responsible your potential
tenant is, as well as their rental history, so that you can spot any
red flags early on. You can also run a criminal history check if you
wish. However, it is important to note that you cannot discrimi-
nate against someone based on their criminal history unless the
crime is related to their past or present tenancy.

Once you have completed all of your screenings and background
checks, you can review what you have learned about your potential tenants and then narrow down the applicants. Once you have a
good number of quality applicants, you can conduct interviews to
see if you get along with your prospective tenants or if there are
any red flags that you might notice when speaking with them. It is
a good idea to plan what you are going to ask them in advance so
that you can accurately compare your potential tenants and ensure
that you are asking the most important questions. If there is
anything concerning that arose in your background checks, you
can also ask them to elaborate, as there may be a valid reason for
it, which could provide you with peace of mind.

There is a lot that goes into building a solid foundation for the
BRRRR method. It is important to do this groundwork to ensure
that whatever steps you take beyond this will have the best chance
of leading you to success. In the next chapter, we will take some
time to explore how incorporating short-term rentals can further
enhance your rental income and investment returns.

FROM DREAM TO REALITY

"Every person who invests in well-selected real estate in a growing section of a prosperous community adopts the surest and safest method of becoming independent, for real estate is the basis of wealth."

— THEODORE ROOSEVELT

Everyone wants financial freedom, but the majority of people have no idea how to achieve it. To them, it will always be a dream—unless, that is, they see just how possible it is. I told you at the beginning of our journey together that I was unsure about real estate investing at first. To begin with, it was just about making sure my family had somewhere to live. It was only when I refinanced that house and used the equity to acquire another property that I realized what I could do with real estate investing.

Real estate is one of the most solid investments you can make, and the return you can get from it is, in most cases, far higher than it is for other forms of investment. I had to prove this to myself before I believed it, but now my goal is to help other people see just how possible it is. I talk to so many people who tell me that they're not wealthy enough to invest in property or that they don't even own their own house so they couldn't possibly consider it. They assume that these things are barriers, which means they don't even look into it.

I want to show people that there are fewer barriers to real estate investing than most people realize. I'm sure you've heard the expression, "Give a man a fish, and you feed him for a day. Teach a man to fish, and you feed him for a lifetime." That's how I view sharing what I know about real estate investment: I want to teach as many people as I can to build their wealth over their lifetime— and you can help me, simply by leaving a short review online.

By leaving a review of this book on Amazon, you'll help new readers to find it and understand that they, too, have the power to make money from real estate.

Anyone who's even slightly curious about whether they could make real estate investing work for them is looking for guidance— and your review will help them to find it. Together, we can help more people to make sure that financial freedom has a chance of becoming a reality instead of remaining a dream. I don't know about you, but that's a world I want to live in.

Thank you so much for your support. Now, let's get back to business!

Scan the QR code below

6

USING AIRBNB TO SUPERCHARGE
RENTAL INCOME

T he global short-term rental market is estimated to be worth $135 billion, reflecting a 9.7% increase from 2019 to 2023 (Achen 2025). This growth highlights the lucrative opportunities available to property owners who effectively leverage platforms like Airbnb. I have personally found success with Airbnb, which has far exceeded my expectations. Once I decided to truly get involved and create a plan, I was able to see significant financial gains through the Airbnb platform, and it is the reason I am so passionate about real estate.

WHEN AIRBNB IS A STRATEGIC CHOICE

When it comes to renting out your property, you don't have to do it solely on a long-term basis. A long-term strategy is great for many people, but you can definitely earn a substantial amount of money through Airbnb and short-term rentals. If you have never considered Airbnb as an option, let this be your sign to at least think about it.

Whether your Airbnb will be successful depends on several factors. Properties located in tourist-heavy areas or near major stadiums and events will have the highest chance of generating a steady income. Since Airbnb is a short-term rental strategy, the goal is to achieve higher occupancy rates, which means more people booking with you over time.

The type of property you have may not matter, as there are many different ways to rent out a property on Airbnb. It offers very flexible options, so you are likely to find one that is best suited to you. Firstly, you could rent out an entire standalone house. This means your guests will have access to the rooms, facilities, amenities, and anything else on the property. This arrangement is quite desirable, as guests enjoy having all the space to themselves, and it provides them with additional privacy.

You could also rent out an apartment or a condo in a larger building or complex. In this case, you would be renting out whatever is in that apartment, such as the rooms, living area, bathrooms, and kitchen. There will also be some shared areas and amenities, such as the laundry room, swimming pools, outdoor amenities, and entrances. Another option is to rent out a private room on Airbnb. This works if you have a space in your home that is not currently being used. Your guests will have their own private room, but they will need to share spaces like the living area, dining area, kitchen, and possibly the bathroom.

The final option is the shared room option, where one bedroom is shared by multiple guests. Think of a dormitory where several people sleep in one room using separate beds or bunk beds. There will also be shared rooms and amenities, such as the bathroom and kitchen. This will be a very affordable option for most guests, but it's not universally appealing, so only those who are on a budget would be attracted to something like this.

As you can see, there are many different options when it comes to renting out an Airbnb. Something good to know is that there are quite a few amenities that stand out from the crowd and make a property even more attractive on the Airbnb platform. Remember, people are booking with Airbnb because they're looking for a short-term rental, either for a vacation, business trip, or some other personal reason. In most cases, they are looking for a comfortable place to stay, and if they are on vacation, they will want some special amenities. A pool or hot tub is a great draw, and people will be willing to pay more for this. Staying with the water theme, if you have a property near the waterfront or with beach access, this is also a great draw. Everybody loves a view of the water, plus there are so many things to do, including water sports or even just relaxing on the beach. Water is not the only thing that attracts people; they also love outdoor and mountain views, so any of those options would be really good locations for an Airbnb.

If you have interesting architecture, a luxury bathroom, or unique amenities, such as a theater room, then these features will also attract more people. In the case of individuals wanting to book an Airbnb for business reasons, having an office space will be key and a significant attraction. What will attract your potential guests depends on their needs and your location. If you're situated in a city center or an economic hub, you are likely to attract more people who are coming to the city for work trips, and catering to them will be important. However, if you have a property that is more on the outskirts, where there are plenty of views, activities, and water attractions, you are likely to attract more people who are there for a vacation.

On Airbnb, you can also advertise experiences, not just property rentals. You can curate specific experiences in your area that potential guests would be excited to participate in, such as rides, city tours, sightseeing tours, and fun activities. You can add these experiences to your Airbnb booking package to make it even more attractive for people looking for a fun holiday experience. You can provide guests with tips and tricks for the area, as well as guide them to restaurants or provide maps of the area where they can go hiking, biking, swimming, or skiing. You might also be able to provide them with locations for museums and historical sites so they can explore while they're in the area. Remember that with Airbnb, you are essentially creating an experience rather than just renting out a place for people to stay. The more effort you put into creating a wonderful experience for your potential guests, the better your chances are of receiving positive reviews and more bookings.

Airbnb is a short-term rental platform, which means that when you engage with it, you'll be involved in short-term rentals. Short-term rentals require significantly more hands-on work and effort because you need to ensure that your guests are well taken care of, and you must prepare the property for the next guests after your current ones check out. There is indeed a lot that goes into managing an Airbnb, which is why I have written two books on this specific topic.

You can find both of my books on Amazon by scanning the QR code:

These books have already helped many people build the Airbnb business of their dreams, so I'm confident they will be useful to you if this is something you are considering as well.

Additionally, I have a Facebook community group specifically for Airbnb and short-term rental owners. This is a great place for people to connect and receive helpful tips and tricks along their Airbnb journey. Feel free to join this group to gain valuable insights and connect with others who are on the same journey as you.

Name: Airbnb Host Community

URL: https://www.facebook.com/groups/airbnbhostcommunity

QR Code:

You can choose to have either a short-term or a long-term rental. Both options have their pros and cons, so it is better to understand these before you choose a strategy. Let's discuss them in more detail.

Short-Term Rentals

For most of this book, we have been discussing long-term rentals or at least considering them as an option. Now we are going to switch gears and talk about the pros and cons of short-term rentals so that you fully understand this method.

Pros

A significant advantage of short-term rentals is that they offer a lot of flexibility. You can decide when you want to rent your property out and when you want to keep it vacant or live in it yourself. For example, if you own a beach cottage that you want to use for family vacations a few weeks a year, you can rent that property out through short-term rentals during the times you are not going to be there. This way, your property does not remain vacant and unused for the majority of the year, but you still have the option to enjoy a vacation home when you want it. This flexibility also allows you to be much more hands-on with your property, enabling you to check and inspect it whenever you need to. This means you can conduct more frequent maintenance checks compared to if someone were living on your property on a long-term basis and would prefer not to be disturbed as often.

Short-term rentals also provide the opportunity to earn significantly more money than long-term rentals. Consider this: When you book a vacation, you pay per night. If you multiply the per-night rate at an average vacation rental by 30 days, this amount would be much greater than what someone would pay for monthly rent at the same property. If your property has a good booking rate, with people staying fairly often, you will definitely be making more money than if you were renting it out on a long-term basis.

Another major benefit is that you are far less likely to encounter legal disputes with a short-term rental than with a long-term one. Tenant rights and laws can lead to lengthy legal disputes, whereas in a short-term rental situation, the guest is only staying for a few days. They are unlikely to have the time to engage in any significant arguments or disagreements that could lead to legal action.

Cons

There are some downsides to short-term rentals that are important to be aware of. One of the biggest risks is the possibility of
long vacancies for the property. You can never truly predict the
market, and there is a chance that your property will not receive as
many bookings as you would like. Additionally, you must take into
consideration the seasonal market and the type of property you
have. If you own a beach vacation home, it is likely that during the
winter, there will be few people interested in booking with you. In
this case, you might experience a season where you do not have
any guests for months on end. There is also significant competition for short-term rentals, and if you have found a good area for
an Airbnb, it is likely that other Airbnbs are in the vicinity.

Since different people are coming in and out of your property all
the time, you must consider the fact that this could result in
increased wear and tear on the amenities and the general structure
of the property. It is also important to recognize that people might
be a bit more careless while on vacation, so the chances of scuffs,
scratches, and other minor damages could increase. You also need
to remember that while you may have a certain standard for how
you like to take care of things or live in a house, this standard may
not be the same for other people. Spills, stains, and damage are all
common and may require you to perform regular maintenance
and refurbishment more often.

Another downside is the risk of neighbor complaints due to
unruly or loud guests. Even if your guests are well-behaved, there
may be inconveniences that you inadvertently cause your neighbors, such as parking congestion or a buildup of dirt and trash.
Since your guests will be staying on a short-term basis, they may
not be familiar with the norms of the neighborhood, which could
lead to behaviors that irritate your neighbors.

With a short-term rental or an Airbnb, you do need a high level of involvement since there is a high turnover rate of guests. You'll have to ensure that the house is cleaned and restocked before your next guest checks in. On top of that, you might also need to be available should there be an issue that a guest needs help with. Remember that you are essentially providing a service to your guests, so being on call is simply part of the job. You want to make sure your guests have the best experience, and this means that you need to assist them when they need it. If not, they might leave a negative review, which could heavily impact your future bookings.

Another thing to consider is that maintenance is much more urgent with a short-term rental because you want to ensure your guests have the best quality stay and that their satisfaction level is high. If there are non-urgent or smaller maintenance tasks, you might be able to schedule them for a later date with a long-term rental, but this is not the case with a short-term rental. Additionally, you can't perform maintenance when your guests are on the property, as this will not go well for your ratings or your overall guest experience. This means that you might need to conduct maintenance by not taking any bookings for a certain period or by scheduling it outside of business hours, which might result in you paying higher fees for your contractors.

Long-Term Rentals

Let's have a look at some of the pros and cons of long-term rentals.

Pros

The huge benefit of a long-term rental is that the income stream is much more predictable. You and your tenant will agree on a rental amount that will be paid to you regularly, and you can expect this amount on a specific payday. This allows you to know how much money is coming in and to budget accordingly. This arrangement is a commitment between you and your tenant, and you can rely on this consistent payment.

Long-term tenants also tend to take better care of the property since they view it as a long-term stay and as their home. This creates a sense of ownership, and they feel responsible for the space. They are also likely to report any maintenance issues quickly so that they can be resolved before escalating into something bigger.

With a long-term rental, there is a lower likelihood of long vacancy periods, and the turnover rate is significantly smaller. This results in much less work for you because you don't have to market the property and find new tenants constantly. Additionally, your tenants will need to give you notice before they pack up and leave, which gives you some time to find new tenants.

Cons

There are a few downsides to long-term rentals that are important to consider. Firstly, there isn't much flexibility when it comes to your property. You won't be able to use your property for personal purposes until the lease agreement has ended. Your tenants have exclusive use of the property, and you have very little control over what occurs. Additionally, you need to respect your tenants' privacy, so you can't always check up on or inspect the property.

You also need to be well-versed in the legal landscape and tenant rights surrounding long-term rentals. If you have problematic tenants, they could use this to their advantage, which could disadvantage you and pose significant challenges. It can be very difficult to evict a tenant, even if they are not paying rent or taking care of the property. There are strict rules and guidelines that you must follow to address these situations, and it could take months or even years to achieve the desired outcome.

Another downside is that you may have to deal with problematic tenants, which can be incredibly time-consuming. Unlike short-term rentals, you don't get to restart with a new group of people after a few days. The issues that arise with long-term rentals stem from the fact that tenant and landlord relationships are much more complex, time-consuming, and resource-intensive. You may need to engage in extensive communication, problem-solving efforts, and negotiations. You might also need to involve other professionals, such as lawyers and property experts, to help resolve the issues. All of this can be incredibly time-consuming and expensive.

Airbnb and short-term rentals, in general, are great strategies for renting out your property to many people. There are some factors you need to consider to ensure that this is something you can handle. It might require significantly more time and effort on your part because you have to manage the property and ensure your guests are happy at all times. However, the positives and benefits are definitely worth it if you have the time and capacity to do this. You can potentially earn much more money with a short-term rental, plus you get the opportunity to meet a variety of interesting people from all around the world. It is crucial to assess your properties and the current market to determine if Airbnb is a suitable avenue for increasing your rental income. You could use Airbnb for one or two of your properties in your real estate portfolio while keeping the others as long-term rentals, allowing you to have a variety of income streams. Ultimately, it is up to you and the strategy you wish to pursue.

In understanding how Airbnb can boost your rental income, it's essential to establish a solid legal and financial foundation. This is important regardless of the rental strategy you use with the BRRRR method. In the next chapter, we will discuss the business structures, financial planning, and legal considerations necessary for long-term success in real estate investing.

PART III

BUILD SMART AND GROW BIG

LET'S TALK LEGAL, FINANCIAL, AND BUSINESS MATTERS

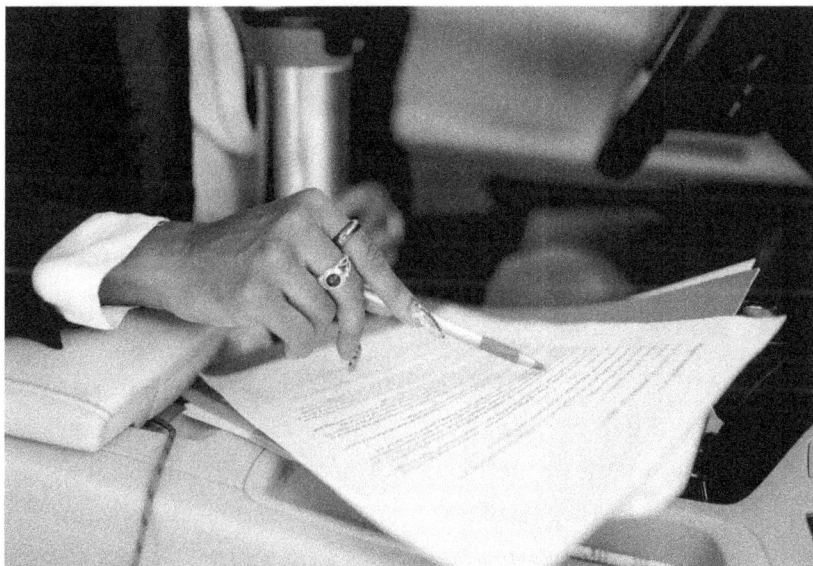

According to the IRS, all rental income must be reported on your tax return, and in general, the associated expenses can be deducted from your rental income (Internal Revenue Service n.d.). This is why it is important to know the ins and outs of legal and financial matters.

CHOOSING THE RIGHT OWNERSHIP STRUCTURE

Choosing the right ownership structure is crucial when you are investing in real estate. Your two main options are individual ownership or LLC ownership, which stands for limited liability company. With individual ownership, it is incredibly simple and involves owning the property in your name. There is less paperwork and administration required for this option. With an LLC, you separate your personal assets from your property or real estate investment. This means that should there be a lawsuit or claim against your property, your personal finances and wealth will be protected. It means that your investment is owned by a separate entity; even though you own that entity, you are not personally liable. If there is a claim or a lawsuit regarding your property, it will go through the LLC rather than your name. Basically, just as if an individual sues a company, the CEO of the company is not personally responsible for paying that claim out of his or her own pocket. It is covered by business expenses, and the business takes care of it separately from any personal assets.

Another thing to consider is the tax implications that come with both methods. When you own a property individually, you will need to file taxes on your rental income as part of your personal tax return. If your properties are under an LLC, there is a completely different way to file your taxes. The income you generate from your properties is not taxed at a corporate level, so you will need to file Form 1065 and then report the income on your individual tax return.

When it comes to how easy it is to use either of these methods, there are definitely advantages and disadvantages to both. For example, if you have the property under individual ownership, you can easily access funds from your bank or financial service provider without the additional work of setting up an LLC.

However, with an LLC, there are additional protections against creditors, plus you can establish a board of directors for better decision-making as your business grows. When you own a property in your personal capacity, there is no protection against personal liability, so you will have to take full responsibility if there is legal action, and your personal assets might be at risk of being repossessed if there are any financial issues.

UNDERSTANDING PERMITS, INSURANCE, AND CONTRACTS

When purchasing a property to renovate or improve, it is important to understand all of the permits and contracts that you will need in order to do so legally and safely. Undertaking these improvements without proper research can put you at risk of engaging in illegal activities, making you liable for fines or even jail time. It is also important to remember that most states and municipalities have different regulations, so you'll need to research your specific area to find out what permit contracts or legal frameworks are in place to ensure compliance. Although the permit process can vary from place to place, some basics are important to understand, regardless of where you live.

Not every small home improvement will require a permit, but larger projects that involve electrical, mechanical, and structural changes will likely need one. Any of these changes must comply with local codes, and you will need a basic plan in place before applying for a permit. Examples of projects that might require a permit include fencing, new windows, plumbing, electrical work, siding, water heaters, and renovations that exceed a certain total cost. Smaller tasks, such as painting, installing new walls, minor electrical work, new countertops, or adding fixtures and faucets, typically do not require a permit.

In addition to obtaining the necessary permits, you should also consider getting insurance to cover your property and renovations. At the end of the day, many things could go wrong, and you don't want to be out of pocket for any unexpected events. Having insurance will protect you and your property, ensuring that you have the funds available to handle emergencies. Unfortunately, there are many instances where an unexpected emergency occurs, and the property owner does not have enough money to address it. In such cases, the property owner may need to sell the property to mitigate their losses, or the property may remain in disrepair for years until the owner can save enough money to continue with the renovations. This results in wasted time and lost revenue, which is definitely something you want to avoid.

There are many different types of insurance available, and if you obtain general home insurance, it might be covered under that umbrella. Looking for some sort of umbrella policy might be your best option because it means that you only have to pay one insurance bill rather than multiple different insurance premiums. It is always a good idea to compare insurance premiums in terms of their cost and the benefits you will receive from them. You also want to ensure that the claims process is straightforward, so look for insurance providers that have good reviews and real-life examples of people being able to access their claims quickly.

As mentioned earlier, many things could go wrong when you own a property. The type of insurance you will obtain depends on the type of property you have as well as your location. In certain areas, there are greater risks for specific issues than in others. For example, some areas have a higher chance of flooding or fires, and in such cases, you want to ensure that your insurance policy covers these and other natural disasters. Other aspects you want your insurance policy to cover include liability, loss of income, and rent guarantee insurance. You should also consider obtaining insurance for workers' compensation and builders' risk insurance, especially if you are undertaking a larger project with many workers on-site. If something were to happen to the workers, you might be liable for their medical expenses, so having this insurance means that it will not come out of your pocket.

You also need to have the right contracts when you are involved in property investment or purchasing a property. There are many different types of contracts available, but there are five that you should consider, which are the most common in this context. The first is a purchase agreement, where the buyer and the seller agree to transfer ownership of a specific property. All the details regarding the sale and transfer of the property will be included in this contract.

The next common type of contract is an assignment contract. This is specifically for wholesaling, as it facilitates the property sale between the current homeowner and a separate buyer who is not the wholesaler.

Another contract is a lease agreement, which is a contract between the tenant and the landlord. This contract outlines the expectations of both parties, as well as the rent that the tenant needs to pay to the landlord.

Power of attorney is another important contract, necessary when the owner of a property grants permission for their attorney or another individual to act as their proxy in the transaction.

The final common contract is a subject-to contract. With this contract, the person buying the property will take over the seller's existing mortgage payment without needing to go through the entire process of obtaining their own mortgage, undergoing a credit check, or making a down payment.

272 | CHAPTER 7

TAXES AND RECORD-KEEPING

Whenever you are earning income, regardless of how or where it is coming from, you need to keep the taxes in mind. You must ensure that you are paying your taxes correctly; otherwise, you could face hefty fees and possible jail time if you are purposely avoiding paying taxes or evading the tax authorities. Unfortunately, taxes are a normal part of society, and we all have to comply, so making sure that we know what we are liable for will benefit us in the long term.

Rental income needs to be reported and taxed, so if you are using the BRRRR method, this is something you need to consider. This type of income is reported by you on Schedule E (Form 1040), though you might receive a Form 1099-MISC from your property manager if they collected rent on your behalf and are required to report it (Internal Revenue Service 2024). If you are filling out your taxes online, the program will automatically prompt you to complete the appropriate forms, such as Schedule E. It is typically a good idea to get someone with experience to assist you with your tax return, especially if you are not familiar with the process. This will help you avoid any mishaps and allow you to save money on your taxes.

Many categories are tax-deductible when you are working with real estate. This is a great benefit, and it's important to know what these deductions are so that you can effectively lower your taxable income and the amount of taxes you will be paying. Some expenses that can be deducted include mortgage interest, property tax, operating expenses, depreciation, and repairs.

It is very important that you keep thorough records of your income, expenses, and any financial transactions related to your property. This will help you with your tax filing process and allow you to analyze your finances. It is recommended that you keep a record for at least three years. You may choose to keep your financial and tax records for longer, just in case, but this is definitely the minimum. When you maintain a record of all your income and expenses, it will make tax preparation much easier because you will have everything on hand. If the IRS requests certain proof or documentation, you can quickly provide it, which will reduce the amount of time you spend going back and forth. It also makes the process significantly less stressful.

In general, you must have documentary evidence, including items such as checks, bills, receipts, and emails that can support your expenses. A good rule of thumb is that if you have spent any money on or for your property, you should keep the evidence of this safely. You can retain hard copies, but you can also scan or take pictures of the hard copies and save them digitally, making it easier to keep track of what you have. Additionally, you can keep a record of any travel expenses related to rental property repairs. You may want to consult a tax professional to find out if there are any other tax deductions you could qualify for. Although hiring a tax professional does incur a cost, they are usually worth it because they can make your life much easier and save you money in the long run by helping you reduce your tax liability.

SETTING UP BUSINESS ACCOUNTS AND SYSTEMS

It is not necessarily mandatory, but it is a good idea to set up separate bank accounts for your property business and your personal account. While it might seem like a tedious process to establish these different accounts, it will definitely be worth it in the long run, as it simplifies your finances and makes tax season much easier for you.

There are numerous benefits to having a separate account for your business or property investments. One is that it prevents the co-mingling of funds. It is easy to let your business and personal funds become mixed, making it difficult to determine which goes where, especially if everything is in one account. When everything is combined, it can be very challenging to track your expenses and report them for financial and tax purposes. Having a clear separation between your accounts simplifies everything, allowing you to prevent overspending in certain areas. It also helps protect your personal assets and funds.

When you have a separate account, your general accounting for your rental property will be much easier because you can easily track your income and expenses. If you need to review your spending, you can be confident that the expenses in your property account are solely for your property and nothing else. This will reduce the overall preparation time when you are preparing for taxes and financial accounting in general.

As your portfolio grows and you acquire more properties, having a separate bank account makes managing your finances significantly easier. You can also establish a separate bank account for each of your properties, allowing you to track how well each one is performing. This will also be beneficial when you apply for financing from lenders, should you wish to refinance a property or purchase another one.

As your portfolio grows, you might want to start hiring people to assist you with certain areas of your business. This could include property management, accounting, or general administrative duties. These individuals will then become part of an employee payroll, and it will be much simpler if there is a separate account from which you pay these employees. You will also be able to pay your vendors from this account, ensuring that you do not overspend in that area. You will know exactly how much money is in your account, how much you have to spend, and what you need to budget for.

In addition to having these separate accounts, you can also utilize accounting software to help automate and streamline financial management. These days, we really do not have to do all the tedious work ourselves; we can use software and apps to assist. This makes everything much easier and provides us with additional insights that might be more difficult to obtain if we were doing everything on our own. Some good options include QuickBooks, AppFolio, Stessa, and Buildium.

BUILDING YOUR REAL ESTATE TEAM

As your real estate portfolio grows, you can't do everything on your own. It becomes incredibly important to bring people onto your team to help you focus on the things that really matter. Additionally, it is always a good idea to seek advice and assistance in various areas of property management and investing. There are many different roles you fill as a real estate investor, and outsourcing some of this workload will greatly assist you in balancing your tasks.

You might not be able to hire people for every single step of the process at the beginning, but you can always start somewhere and build your team as you progress. One of the first individuals or groups you can bring on board is a driver. This is not someone who will drive you around, but rather someone who will help you find properties that meet your investment criteria. This approach provides you with more options, increasing your chances of finding the right property.

The great thing about this role is that you don't necessarily have to hire a professional to fulfill it. When you first start out, consider reaching out to friends and family members who could be your initial drivers. All you need to do is inform them that you are looking for a specific property that meets your ideal criteria. If they are on the lookout for such properties, they can funnel any leads they find to you, allowing you to decide whether to pursue those options. As you continue your real estate investing journey, you will be able to recruit more drivers who will help you maintain a pipeline of potential property investments.

The next person you can bring on board is called a lead manager. This individual will take the leads provided by the drivers and call around to find the most qualified leads. They will gather more information about the properties that have come their way to identify which ones will be the best fit for you and your goals. It is important for this person to have good interpersonal skills, as they will be interacting with many people while discovering more about the properties.

You might also need an acquisitions manager, who is responsible for closing deals and acquiring the properties. They will receive information from the lead manager and then analyze the properties to determine how much you can offer. They need to possess excellent negotiation skills as well as a solid understanding of the real estate market. This knowledge will help them make better deals and understand what is realistic. The next step involves someone called a disposition manager, who handles the sale of the property after you have flipped and revamped it. They will work to sell your property to a list of qualified buyers to ensure that the sale goes through quickly. If you are not looking to sell the property, then you do not specifically need this person.

Another key member of your team would be a marketing manager or a marketing lead. Since you are on the hunt for new properties and also trying to sell your current properties, marketing will be crucial. Marketing can require a lot of time and effort, especially if you have multiple properties. They will assist by designing your marketing initiatives and working on strategies and plans to help promote your properties. They will also play a key role in attending networking events and conferences to meet more people who could potentially bring in additional leads.

On top of what we have just discussed, there are some other really important members of your team that you will need to get on board. This will include a lender who will provide you with funds while you are in the property market and looking to purchase properties. While you can apply for loans and go through banks and other avenues, having a lender or someone you know you can work with easily will greatly improve the process. Mutual trust will allow things to go more smoothly. If you have a designated person you know you can approach when you need a loan or some extra money, it will be beneficial.

You will also need a real estate agent to assist you with buying and selling properties, as well as a contractor who will help with building and renovating your property. Another important person will be an accountant who will handle the financial and tax aspects.

Some honorable mentions in terms of people you might want on your team include property managers who will manage the day-to-day operations of your property if you cannot do it yourself. They will handle the tenants and the individuals who work on the property daily, so you do not have to be on-site all the time. You might also want to consider getting an appraiser, inspector, or real estate attorney on board. Finally, consider hiring an insurance agent you can trust to help you obtain the best insurance products.

A lot goes into being an investor in real estate, and it's important to have all the finer details sorted out as soon as possible. You'll need to establish an appropriate ownership structure, understand the legal requirements, and maintain accurate financial records to ensure that your business is running at its optimum capacity. You might also want to bring on more people to assist you in areas where you may not be fully competent or where you simply need help. Once you have all of these in place, it will form a foundation for the next step, which is considering how you want to exit your investments effectively. This is exactly what we will be discussing in the next chapter.

EXIT STRATEGIES AND LONG-TERM PLANNING

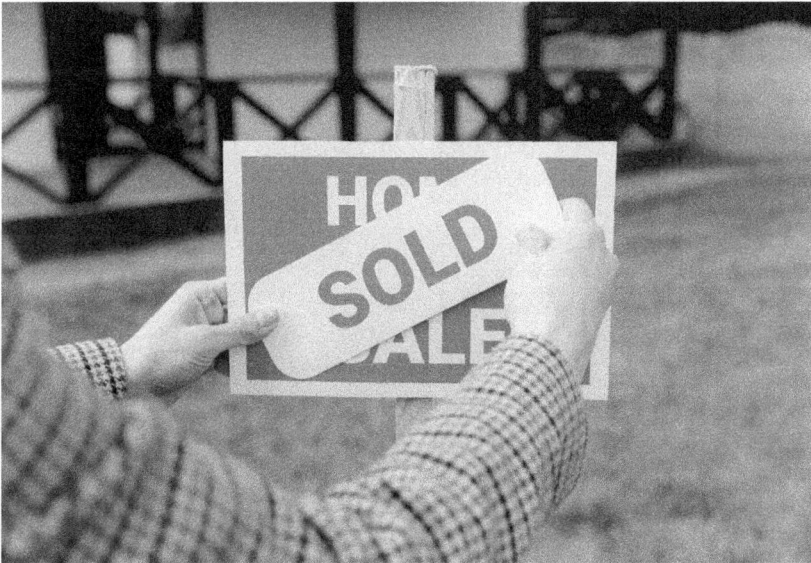

C urrent data from CBRE and NCREIF indicates that over 68% of real estate investors in Q1 2025 revised their exit strategy within 18 months of acquisition (The Luxury Playbook 2025). This highlights the importance of having an exit strategy and adapting it to ensure that it remains effective in the current market and your specific situation. The real estate market is constantly changing, which means we sometimes need to be flexible with our plans regarding the properties we purchase. You might have acquired a property for a specific reason, such as renting it out, but upon further inspection and additional research, you may discover that this is not a renter's market. Consequently, you might need to sell your property or consider another strategy to profit from your investment.

TO SELL OR REFINANCE

When you are involved in real estate investment, you have a choice between mortgage refinancing and selling the property. Both options come with their own pros and cons, so it is important to understand your goals and what you hope to achieve. You also need to assess the housing market to determine which option will suit you better. While refinancing may have been your original plan, you might come to realize that selling could offer more benefits. It is always best to keep an open mind when investing in real estate, as circumstances can change, and you want to be flexible enough to achieve the best results.

Mortgage Refinancing Pros and Cons

When you refinance your property, you are essentially replacing your current mortgage with a new one. The monthly payment you make will now be applied to the new mortgage. There are many different refinancing options available, each with varying rates and terms. If you are using the BRRRR method, you will need to refinance your properties at some point. There are definite benefits to refinancing, including a lower interest rate, debt consolidation, and the opportunity to make home improvements.

When you refinance, you also have to take into consideration a few negatives or drawbacks that come with it. For example, you need a good credit score in order to secure a favorable rate on your refinance. If not, you will find it very difficult to obtain a new loan, which might even end up costing you more money. If you take a cash-out refinance, this can lower the equity in your home, which can be a significant disadvantage, especially if overall housing market prices decrease. Finally, another major downside to consider is that refinancing extends your debt timeline, meaning that you will need to pay back money for a longer period than you might have initially anticipated.

Selling Pros and Cons

Selling your home is another option you can explore. There are many reasons you might choose to sell your property, even if you are currently trying to implement the BRRRR method. This could be because you realize that the home is not generating the amount of money you expected, or perhaps you have too many properties in your portfolio, making it difficult for you to manage them.

One of the biggest benefits of selling your house is that you gain access to immediate funds as soon as the sale goes through. You receive a lump sum, and then you can do what you wish with that money. It also allows you to reduce your overall debt because you can sell your house, pay off your debts, and then take the profit from the sale. If you have owned your property for a significant amount of time or have improved it to the point where it has increased in value, you can sell your house for a much larger profit margin.

The downsides of selling your house include market-dependent value. This means that, because the housing market is always fluctuating, if you choose to sell your house when the market is low, you will receive a lower price than what you deserve or desire. Another factor to consider is that you will need to have your home reappraised if you want to sell, and this comes with additional costs. Selling also means dealing with uncertain timelines. Sometimes houses sell in a matter of days, while in other cases, it can take months or even years to sell. If you're looking to make quick money from selling your property, this may not be possible depending on the current market demand.

There are many reasons people choose to sell rather than rent, even if they are following the BRRRR method. Life can be unpredictable, and it's important to adjust your goals or priorities accordingly. For example, if you have financial goals and have determined that refinancing will not help you achieve them, then selling might be the better option. Perhaps your rental property is not generating much income, making it less worthwhile to keep. In cases where you co-own property with someone else and there is a death, divorce, separation, or a general partnership dispute, it might be better to sell so that everyone can recoup their investment rather than attempting to maintain a joint rental. Another reason people consider selling is if there is a significant issue with the property that will require too much time and resources to resolve. As you can see, there are many reasons to sell your property, and it all depends on your current situation and your goals.

UTILIZING 1031 EXCHANGES AND UNDERSTANDING TAX IMPLICATIONS

A 1031 exchange is a process that allows an investor to defer capital gains tax when selling an investment property. This is permitted because the proceeds are reinvested into another property that is very similar to the one being sold. Essentially, it is a swap from one property to another. While this may sound like an excellent idea since you do not have to pay the capital gains tax immediately, the truth is that it can be very difficult to find a similar property to the one you currently own. You also need to ensure that the new property is located in an area you like and meets all your other requirements, even if it is similar and qualifies.

There are some timing rules that come into play with the 1031 exchange. The first is the 45-day rule, which indicates that once the property has been sold, the intermediary entity will receive the money. As the seller, you will not be able to accept the cash immediately; otherwise, it will jeopardize the 1031 treatment. Within the 45 days, you must designate the property you are replacing your current one with in writing. You can designate up to three properties, as long as you intend to close on one of them. In some cases, you may designate more than three. The other rule is the 180-day rule, which requires you to close on your new property within 180 days after selling your previous property. You can also purchase a replacement property before selling the one you currently own and still qualify for this exchange, but the same 45- and 180-day time windows will apply.

If you engage in a 1031 exchange, you will need to report this to the IRS. You must submit Form 8824 along with your tax return for the year in which the exchange occurred. In this form, you will need to provide descriptions of both properties, the dates they were transferred, and your relationship with the person or people with whom you exchanged properties. You will also need to indicate the value of each property.

One important tax implication to be aware of is depreciation recapture. This occurs when the IRS collects tax on the depreciation you claimed after selling your assets for more than their book value. Within this category, there are two types of properties you might need to calculate: 1245 property and 1250 property.

Using Section 1245 property includes the depreciation of the property when calculating the profit from its sale. Let's say you bought a property for $100,000, and each year you claim $10,000 as depreciation deductions, which means you are lowering your taxable income by $10,000 every year. After five years, you would have claimed $50,000, making your adjusted cost basis $50,000. This is because you subtracted the amount you have deducted over the five years from the original cost. Let's say that in this scenario, the housing market is really bad, and when you sell your property, you sell it for only $70,000. This might seem like a loss because you originally spent $100,000 on the property when you first bought it, but the IRS calculates things differently. Instead of comparing it to the original sale price, they adjust the value of the property based on the deductions. So, if the new value is $50,000 and you sold it for $70,000, it means that you have made a $20,000 profit. That $20,000 is subject to depreciation recapture, which means that you will be paying your regular income tax rate on that amount.

The next topic we will cover is Section 1250 gains. With this, the real estate investor benefits from a favorable depreciation recapture, as business equipment is taxed separately at a regular income rate, while real estate depreciation recapture is capped at 25%. To qualify for this, you will need to use straight-line depreciation. This means you will need to claim equal deductions every year over the lifespan of your property. When it comes time to sell your property and you sell it for more than the original price, the final sale price will be divided into two parts. The profit you make up to the amount of depreciation you've already claimed in previous years is subject to a maximum recapture rate of 25%. The profit that exceeds the original purchase price will be taxed at a lower long-term capital gains rate, which is around 15% for most people.

Speaking of capital gains, it is important to understand what they are and how they impact your taxes. Capital gains tax is simply the tax imposed on the profit after you have sold your property or any other asset. You have made gains from your investment, and those gains need to be taxed as profit since they qualify as income. Using the 1031 exchange is a good way to lower your capital gains tax, but there are also other strategies, including converting your second home into your main residence or investing in Opportunity Zones, which are designated areas that offer tax benefits for real estate investors. It is always a good idea to consult with an accountant or tax practitioner to help you minimize the amount you will pay in capital gains tax so that you can save as much money as possible.

BUILDING A SUSTAINABLE REAL ESTATE PORTFOLIO AND SCALING UP

As you continue on this real estate journey, you will want to ensure that you are building a sustainable real estate portfolio—something that lasts for a long time and continues to generate income. A strong portfolio will help establish a solid financial foundation for you, even in the face of changes in the housing market.

When building your real estate investment portfolio, it is important to have a long-term perspective so that you can set your objectives and goals correctly. Doing this will help streamline your choices as you begin to build your portfolio. You must know where you are going before you start taking steps to get there. Consider factors such as how much time you can dedicate to your real estate investment portfolio and the amount of work or effort you are willing to invest.

Once you know what you want to achieve from your real estate investing, it's time to choose a starting point. For first-time investors, it is crucial not to try to do too much at once. Even if you have the finances to invest in multiple properties, it is best to start small so that you can acclimate to real estate investing and understand its implications for your lifestyle. Starting small also allows you to gain a good understanding of real estate before committing to something larger. You might consider options like house hacking, as it is easier to qualify for a loan in this scenario and can help you pay off the main property in which you reside.

The next step is to consider how you will grow your portfolio. While it may seem appealing to expand your portfolio annually by continuously adding properties, exponential growth is far more advantageous. It demonstrates a greater increase over time. Linear growth involves investing in rental properties of the same or similar value every few years; while this approach will yield growth, it may take some time before you see anything substantial. However, if you create a portfolio that grows exponentially, you can use your rental income to leverage and accumulate more equity, allowing you to purchase additional properties that generate more income. This is the beauty of the BRRRR method. It enables you to leverage your investments and increase your income over time. Consequently, you will be able to acquire more properties in a shorter period, resulting in significantly higher profits.

If you want to have an edge in the real estate game, it is essential that you fully understand your local real estate market. This is especially important while you are still growing your real estate portfolio. If you are considering purchasing properties that are very far away from you, the truth is that you don't always know what's happening in your rental home or what is going on in the neighborhood. This poses challenges when you are trying to make decisions about your real estate investments, and there may be things that you are missing. If you keep your real estate investments in areas that you know well and can easily travel to, it will be much easier for you to keep track of things and ensure that you are getting the most out of your real estate investment. It is also easier to monitor your local market because you are there, and it will interest you since it impacts you personally, not just in your investment space.

As your real estate investment portfolio starts to grow, it is crucial to understand that diversification is key. When you diversify your real estate investments, you essentially protect yourself while maximizing your returns. A non-diversified portfolio is one in which you are only investing in one type of real estate or property. For example, you might only invest in apartments that are close to the city center. When you diversify, you spread your investment across different types of properties and locations. This is important because if something were to happen with one type of investment or property, it would not impact your entire portfolio as severely, since you have many different types within your portfolio. In the example where you own three apartments in the city center, if something were to happen to the city and it no longer becomes a popular place to live, you would essentially lose your revenue from all three of your investments. However, if you invest in a multifamily home in the suburbs, one apartment in the city, and an Airbnb vacation rental, even if something happens to the apartment in the city, the other two investments in your portfolio will still be generating income, so you will remain secure.

A good rule of thumb for diversification is the 60/20/20 rule. This is where you have 100% of your portfolio divided into three smaller categories. You can split it up however you like, but traditionally, 60% of your portfolio is allocated to multifamily residential properties, 20% goes to vacation rentals, and the last 20% is for private equity real estate funds. With this kind of diversification, you get the best of all worlds in real estate investing. You invest in long-term and short-term real estate, as well as funds, all of which have different levels of profit generation and security. You don't have to stick to these ratios, and it's best to find something that works best for you, but this is definitely a great starting point as you try to diversify your investment portfolio.

COMMON MISTAKES TO AVOID

There are many mistakes that you could make or be making when investing in real estate. Understanding these common mistakes early can help you avoid them as you move through this journey. If you know to expect something that could cause a problem down the line, you will recognize it quickly, and you might not have to deal with it at all. Let's talk about some of the most common mistakes when it comes to real estate investing.

Underestimating Costs

Underestimating the total cost of a house flip or rental is a very common mistake. It is easy to miscalculate the overall costs of renovating a house if you have not done it before. There are many things you might not think about until you reach the point where you need them. This is why it is important to conduct thorough research. You can also obtain quotes and appraisals to ensure you know what the costs will be. Then, you'll need to create a detailed budget and do your best to stick to it throughout the process.

Not Doing Enough Research

Research is a crucial step when you are going to invest a significant amount of your money in something. If you don't conduct your research properly, it could lead to bigger issues down the road. For example, if you don't research the city or area you are buying in and that area is in decline, you could end up unable to sell or rent out your property for as much as you would like when the time comes. Remember to conduct market research as well as research on contractors, materials, and anything else you might think is necessary.

Choosing the Wrong Location

When it comes to property, location will always be one of the most important factors to consider. People typically want to move to a specific area and then look for their dream house; it's not the other way around. Finding an area that is safe, clean, and easily accessible is crucial. You also want to ensure that the neighborhood has increasing or stable property values, as this improves your chances of getting the amount you want when you sell your property. If you can find an up-and-coming neighborhood or area, it will be a great benefit to you because it means you can buy at a lower rate and have a greater chance of making a profit.

Over-Improving the Property

Yes, there is such a thing as over-improving your property. This means that you are making more improvements than are necessary to achieve a good profit. Certain improvements will yield a good return on investment, while others, although nice, are not as worthwhile. When you are making an investment, every step you take needs to be aligned with your end goal. You want to maximize your profit while minimizing your expenses. This is not about cutting corners; rather, it is about being smart with your money to ensure that you are making worthwhile changes.

Rushing the Process (Timeline)

We all want to get things done as quickly as possible, but when it comes to real estate, it is not advisable to rush the process. This is especially true when renovating your property. Rushed work can lead to mistakes and problems that will cost you significantly to fix down the line. Quality will always be more important than speed. While you do not want things to be delayed unnecessarily, taking your time with each step is crucial to ensure that you are doing everything thoroughly.

Not Having an Exit Strategy

It is essential to have an exit strategy because you do not want to hold on to a property longer than necessary or end up selling it for a much lower price than you intended. Lost profit can lead to larger financial problems, especially if you have a strict budget or specific financial goals to achieve. Before purchasing a house to flip, make sure you have considered an exit strategy. This could involve selling the property if you are unable to find the right tenant, or if you have flipped the property and cannot find buyers, you might consider renting it out for some income. This way, you have a backup plan in case things do not work out as you had planned.

Not Enough Patience

A true professional is someone who takes their time to wait for the right property and the right buyer. It can be very tempting to rush through things, but this is not a good long-term strategy. Just because a house is cheap and the current owners appear desperate to sell does not mean that it will be a good buy for you. Remember to practice patience and take a breather between big decisions so that you know you aren't rushing into things.

It is crucial to understand your investment strategies and to reevaluate them from time to time to ensure they remain relevant in the current environment and real estate market. Consider implementing a few of the methods and suggestions we have discussed in this chapter to help you grow your investment business sustainably. Long-term planning is essential, and the next step is to put all of your knowledge into action. In the next chapter, we will discuss executing your first real estate investment deal to set your future up for success.

YOUR FIRST DEAL

My first deal wasn't anything flashy or massive. We were new immigrants, so we did not have a lot of disposable income to purchase the best properties in desirable areas. We bought an old, rundown house in the countryside because it was all we could afford. My wife and I had a newborn baby, and I had started a new job, so there was a lot we were still trying to figure out. The house needed a lot of work, but we were ready to roll up our sleeves and do most of the renovations ourselves. This included tasks such as installing new floors, building a new kitchen and laundry room, painting, replacing the doors, and landscaping the garden.

My little family lived in this house for two years before we decided to get the property revalued. I originally bought the house for $282,000 and paid a 20% deposit. The rest was financed through a mortgage. Once the property was revalued, it was worth $345,000, which meant we had gained quite a bit of equity in just two years. From there, I decided to refinance and was able to borrow up to 80% of the new value. This meant I could borrow $276,000. The refinance replaced the original mortgage and gave us about $50,000 in cash-out equity. This amount was perfect for a deposit on a two-bedroom apartment, and we still had some money left over, so we decided to refinish the apartment and run it as a short-term rental. This marked the true start of my real estate investing journey and how I got into Airbnb.

If I'm being honest, those first couple of years didn't truly feel like I was making a real estate investment. I was just trying to make the best of my situation by improving the home where I lived. This hard work really paid off and became a catalyst for my real estate investment journey. My family and I took the first step and started small. We learned as we went along and chose to reinvest whatever we earned. These small steps made a huge difference in the long run. I gained momentum, and I used this to keep going. Eventually, my property portfolio grew one deal at a time. I know that if I hadn't taken that first step with my very first house and then purchased that apartment, I would never be where I am today. One smart move in the right direction is all it takes to change the entire game.

STAYING MOTIVATED WHEN DEALS GO WRONG

Even with the best-laid plans, a deal can still go wrong, or the market might not work in your favor. Even people who have been in the real estate game for decades can go through seasons when things are just not working out for them. You will likely face challenges for many reasons; some of them will be within your control, while others won't be. Regardless, it is essential to keep yourself motivated during hard times.

The first thing you need to do is control the things that you can. When things are not working out the way you wanted them to, it is important to understand what you can change and what you can't. If you have made a mistake or miscalculation, this is something you can fix going forward, and you don't have to deal with this bad patch for too much longer. For example, take a look at all of your listings and see if you are overpricing them for the market. Remember that the market changes all the time, and just because something has historically worked does not mean it will continue to do so forever. You might need to adjust your pricing strategy to attract more people to your properties.

It is also a good idea to examine your listings and see if there are any issues that are making them hard to sell. This might relate to how your listings are marketed or to the properties themselves. Perhaps there is something that is dissuading people from renting or buying from you. Put yourself in the shoes of a potential renter or buyer and view things from their perspective. You can even ask a friend, family member, or a completely impartial third party to review your listings and see if anything stands out as a red flag. If you identify any issues, you can make the necessary changes to make your listings more attractive.

Let's say you have checked your properties and have done all the work to ensure that your listings and properties are as attractive as possible. However, you are still not receiving the interest you had hoped for. In this case, it could simply be a rough patch, and it's something you just have to ride out until the market picks up and you can gain momentum once again. If you've been in the real estate game long enough, you will quickly notice that there will be a few times when you encounter these rough patches, and all you need to do is stay motivated until the wave is over. Things will definitely pick up again and return to normal, or even improve beyond normal.

While you're waiting for things to return to an optimal level for your investments, you can work on your mindset. The first step toward cultivating a more positive mindset is to figure out your "why." You've probably heard something along these lines before, but it's such a key part of anything you are trying to achieve. The goal is to uncover the deep reasoning behind your decision to embark on this journey in the first place. Sometimes, it can be easy to forget why we are doing something when we are in the thick of a problem. Reflecting on the beginning, when you first started, will help reawaken some of that passion and fire. Perhaps you wanted to start real estate investing to become financially free or independent. Maybe you want to create a better life for your family and children. Or perhaps you want to have enough money to retire early. Whatever your reasoning or your "why," write it down and keep it with you so that you have something to refer back to each day or when things get difficult.

The next thing you need to do is avoid any negativity from people who are either not in the field or who are simply glass-half-empty types. Whenever you are trying to achieve something great, there will always be individuals who have their own biases and negativity that they want to share with you. Such negativity can easily derail you and make you think the situation is far worse than it actually is. If there are negative people around you, it is an indication that you should not share your strategies or struggles with them. Of course, it is important to have people with whom you can bounce around ideas, but if someone is merely negative and not helping you find solutions, then that person is not the right ally for you. You don't have to cut them off completely, but you should distance yourself from them regarding your real estate investments and that aspect of your life. It is important to find someone who is positive and uplifting in that space to help you stay motivated and keep moving forward.

It might also be worthwhile to examine your current goals and see if they are realistic for where you are right now. If you are feeling like a failure, it could be that your goals do not align with the reality of your situation, making you feel worse than you should. By reevaluating your goals and making them a bit more realistic, you will feel as though you are making progress and actually reaching them, rather than feeling that you keep falling short.

Remember that anyone who has achieved greatness in any sphere of life has faced challenges. Challenges are completely normal, and they can provide a great learning experience if you allow them to. You may be in a difficult situation right now, but you will push through and emerge stronger on the other side if you keep going and maintain a positive outlook. You can look at other people's success stories to see how they have overcome struggles and what they did to build themselves up when times were tough. As you read about others' real estate investment journeys, you will quickly notice that everyone encounters some sort of bump in the road or challenge. Mindset is everything when it comes to reaching your goals and finding success.

THE 90-DAY ACTION PLAN

Having a 90-day plan will provide you with structure, allowing you to clearly work toward your first deal. This plan will serve as a guideline to help you take action. It can be all too easy to read something in a book and, once you reach the final page, fail to apply the information you have learned. A solid plan will help you move forward and allow you to see results. You can modify this action plan as you see fit, but make sure to create a plan for yourself and stick to it. You will find that you learn much more about real estate and investing simply by being active in the field.

Month 1

In the first month, the focus will be on research and analysis. This is what we discussed in the first part of this book. Feel free to revisit that section for a refresher on how to take action during the research and analysis phase. In this phase, you will do your best to thoroughly research the different types of investing and decide which one you want to pursue. Consider writing a pros and cons list tailored to your situation to help you determine which real estate investment strategy aligns with your goals and lifestyle.

You can further deepen your understanding of what you have already learned in this book by researching online and exploring the opinions of others. If you have joined my Airbnb Facebook group, you can ask for advice there or simply read what others have to say and see how you can apply it to your own plan or strategy. Additionally, you can attend real estate investing seminars or networking events to enhance your knowledge and skills, as well as to meet others in the same field.

It is also a good idea to create a simple matrix that includes several factors. You will use this matrix to compare each investment style, helping you understand which one is best suited for you. You can include as many factors as you like, but the four recommended factors are the pros of the strategy, the cons of the strategy, the minimum investment required, and the time commitment involved. Once you have completed this matrix, you can start comparing and identifying which option best suits your needs.

	Pros	Cons	Minimum Investment Needed	Time Required
Strategy 1				
Strategy 2				
Strategy 3				
Strategy 4				

Month 2

In month two, it is time for you to choose your tools. It is important that you select the right ones because, as they say, a builder is only as good as his tools. Choosing the right tools to work with will make your life much easier and more efficient. They will need to align with your overall goals and strategy.

Since there are so many tools available, it is essential for you to conduct some comparisons to help you make a decision. You can also create a matrix to compare different factors and then decide from there. Again, you can include as many factors as you deem fit, but the following are recommended: features, upfront investment, recurring investment, learning curve, and potential ROI.

	Features	Upfront Investment	Recurring Investment	Learning Curve	Potential ROI
Tool 1					
Tool 2					
Tool 3					
Tool 4					

Once you have completed the tools matrix, you will need to choose which ones you want to pursue. You do not need to have a large variety; rather, pick a few that will truly make the biggest impact on your real estate investment journey. You can always add more to your list as your portfolio grows or as you need them. Many tools require you to pay some kind of subscription, so you don't want to commit to too many while you are still in the beginning stages. Reach out to people who have a similar investment style and see if they have any recommendations, and ask how they use them. Also, remember to give yourself some time to learn how to use these tools effectively and navigate any of the platforms you will be using. Some have a steeper learning curve than others, so don't forget to allow yourself that time to learn before you need to use them.

Month 3

In the third month, you will be making your very first deal. This is where the rubber meets the road, and you will do your best to make your first investment. You have all the information from your research and your tools, so now it is time for you to get moving and try to close a deal. With the BRRRR method, the goal is to find a property to purchase so that you can renovate it and then rent it out. At this stage, you need to be on the hunt for the right property. This might mean getting on the phone and making calls or scouring the internet to see what your options are. You might even need to jump in your car and drive around your neighborhood to see what is actually happening in the area and if any potential properties catch your eye.

Commit to doing something each day toward meeting your goal. This way, you maintain momentum and ensure that you don't lose what you have built up. Make notes about what you are doing and how it is turning out for you. For example, if you are pursuing the right property, start writing down exactly what is being said and how you are being received by others. Making these notes is crucial at the beginning because it will help you identify patterns that may or may not be working, allowing you to change your approach or lean into a positive aspect.

You may not close your very first deal within the 90-day or three-month period, and that is completely okay. The goal of having this plan in place is to provide you with something to work toward and to help you build the habit of taking action. Once you reach the end of your 90 days, reevaluate your plan and assess how far you have come. You may have closed a deal, or you may not have; if you have, that's fantastic! If you did not manage to close a deal or find the right property, it doesn't mean you have to go all the way back to the drawing board. You can simply review your journal as well as the matrix you used while researching and discovering. This will provide in-depth information to help you make better decisions in the future and possibly create a more effective strategy.

Real estate investing is an exciting journey, and now that you have reached this point, you have a clear action plan. Congratulations! This is where things start to happen, and you get to see your knowledge transform into action. At this point, you are equipped to begin your real estate investing journey, and you are at one of the most exciting moments in your life. Real estate changed my life, and I'm sure it will do the same for you.

SHARE THE OPPORTUNITY!

Your journey is just beginning, but you still have a chance to help others out on theirs. If you take just a few minutes to leave a short review, you'll help them find it and launch their adventure with real estate investments.

Simply by sharing your honest opinion of this book and a little about your own experience, you'll inspire new readers to try it out for themselves—and you'll show them exactly where they can find all the information they need to get started.

JUST ONE CLICK!

Thank you so much for your support. I wish you every success in your ventures.

Scan the QR code to leave a review.

CONCLUSION

When I first started out as a young real estate investor, I don't think I fully understood how much it was going to change my life. I had seen other people invest in real estate, and it was something that definitely piqued my interest. However, I did not know where to start. It took me a long time to find my footing, and eventually, I began to gain traction. The more I engaged in it, the more I developed a passion for real estate investing. Then the BRRRR method came along, and I knew that this was something I needed to get involved in.

This is probably where you are in your journey. It's the exciting beginning phase, where there is so much opportunity and possibility in front of you. It is time for you to harness this feeling and the knowledge you have already gained from this book and take steps forward to build a better future for yourself and your family. Regardless of what your goals are, investing in real estate is a powerful tool to help you achieve them. Keeping the end goal in mind is what will keep you motivated as you progress through your real estate investment journey.

Remember that, regardless of what you do, the most important thing is to build a solid foundation. Learning, researching, and absorbing as much knowledge as you can is a crucial step. This will help you create a solid plan as you move forward with your investments. It will also enable you to recognize any red flags or potential problems because you have this knowledge tucked away in your memory bank. Even though it might not be the most exciting part of the process, it is crucial, and you shouldn't skip it. One challenge I like to set for myself is to read one article or watch one video about real estate investing every day. This way, I keep the information fresh in my mind, and it helps me reorient my brain back to what is truly important. On top of that, it helps me gain more knowledge about the market, even though I'm only spending a short amount of time each day on this knowledge-seeking. Try it out and see if it works for you.

As much as building up your knowledge bank is important, it is also essential for you to take action. If all you do is learn, read, and research, then you will never reach the point where you actually move forward and purchase your first investment property. It can be scary because it is such a significant financial commitment, but it is something you need to do if you want to become a successful real estate investor. Trust your instincts and the knowledge you have, and you will do great. Remember to surround yourself with people who are more experienced in this area and seek their advice whenever you need it. This will help you continue to grow and avoid common mistakes that many other investors might have made. It is never a bad idea to expand your circle and network, so make sure you are doing your best to build a strong team.

There are many moving parts when it comes to real estate investing and the BRRRR method. It can seem overwhelming to juggle everything, but once you take one small step and continue taking other small steps afterward, you will see that it is not that difficult. You will start to build momentum, and once you have your first property rented out and leverage that to acquire your second property, you will gain a good understanding of this method and how to use it going forward. You are about to embark on an exciting journey, and I know you will do well. It all begins with a single deliberate step and embracing the process. Remember to stay committed to your goals and let each experience propel you toward financial freedom and lasting success. I sincerely wish you nothing but success and happiness as you start investing in real estate and making your dreams come true.

GLOSSARY

1031 Exchange: This allows for tax to be deferred by selling a property and using that money to buy a new property without paying capital gains tax on the sale.

Appraisal: An estimate of the value of a property provided by a professional.

Appreciation: The increase in the value of a property or another investment over time.

ARV: After-Repair Value, the estimated value of a particular property once renovations are completed.

BRRRR: A real estate investment strategy that stands for Buy, Rehab, Rent, Refinance, and Repeat.

Cash Flow: The income generated from rent after subtracting expenses.

Cash-Out Refinance: A type of refinancing where you take out a new mortgage for more than what you currently owe and pocket the extra cash to use as needed.

Closing Costs: Fees that are due at the end of the property purchase process.

Contractor: A person who is hired to perform repairs and renovations on a property.

Credit Score: A three-digit number that shows how well someone manages debt. Lenders use it to evaluate loan eligibility and determine borrowing terms.

Debt-to-Equity Ratio: A way to measure financial risk by comparing how much debt is owed on a property to how much equity (ownership value) the owner has.

Deed: A document that allows a property to be transferred from one owner to another.

Due Diligence: A period just before finalizing the sale of a property during which an investigation takes place.

Equity: The difference between the market value and the amount owed on the property.

Exit Strategy: The plan for making a profit from a real estate investment without retaining ownership.

Flipping: Buying a property, fixing it up, and selling it again in a short time with the goal of making a profit.

Individual Ownership: When one person owns a property outright, with complete control and full responsibility for it.

Interest Rate: A percentage fee that is charged on a loan.

Leverage: To use a loan or credit to purchase a piece of real estate.

LLC (Limited Liability Company): A business structure that lets you own real estate while protecting your personal assets from potential risks or lawsuits.

LTV: This stands for loan-to-value ratio and is used to calculate the potential risk of a loan compared to the value of the property.

MLS (Multiple Listing Service): A shared database where real estate agents list properties for sale, making it easier for buyers and sellers to connect.

Opportunity Zones: Designated areas that offer tax benefits for real estate investors.

Property Manager: A person who is hired to manage a rental property, including tenants, maintenance, and the general day-to-day operations of the property.

Real Estate Agent: A professional with the necessary licenses to assist with buying and selling properties.

Refinance: A method of recovering your capital on a property by replacing your current loan with another one that potentially offers better terms and interest rates.

ROI: Return on Investment, a percentage or ratio that indicates how profitable an investment is or will be.

REFERENCES

Achen, P. 2025. "2024 Vacation Rental Stats Roundup." Rent Responsibly, March 3. https://www.rentresponsibly.org/2024-vacation-rental-stats-roundup/.

Airbnb. n.d. "Success Stories." Accessed July 3, 2025. https://www.airbnb.co.za/resources/hosting-homes/t/success-stories-27?locale=en&_set_bev_on_new_domain=1750448390_EAZjk5MmEyMmJiMT.

Akins, H. 2024. "Spring Cleaning: What Rental Property Documents to Keep, What to Toss, and When." REI Hub, August 26. https://www.reihub.net/resources/rental-property-document-retention/.

All Property Management. 2024. "Landlord's Guide to Rental Property Accounting." December 12. https://www.allpropertymanagement.com/blog/post/landlord-rental-property-accounting/.

Allred, C. 2025. "How to Choose the Right Real Estate Broker." *Investopedia*, April 29. https://www.investopedia.com/updates/real-estate-broker/.

AmeriMac Appraisal Management. 2024. "Can Your Neighborhood Affect Your Property Appraisal? Key Factors to Consider." August 13. https://www.amerimacmanagement.com/about/blog/can-your-neighborhood-affect-your-property-appraisal-key-factors-to-consider/.

Araj, V. 2024. "House Hacking Incorporates a Variety of Ways You Can Use Your House to Pay Living Expenses. Learn What House Hacking Is and How You Can Make It Work for You." Rocket Mortgage, April 3. https://www.rocketmortgage.com/learn/house-hacking.

ArchEyes Team. 2023. "Home Renovations You Shouldn't DIY: A Guide to Professional Help." ArchEyes, September 24. https://archeyes.com/home-renovations-you-shouldnt-diy-a-guide-to-professional-help/.

Ashton, D. 2024. "What Is the BRRRR Method (and How Does It Work)?" University of the Built Environment, September 9. https://www.ube.ac.uk/whats-happening/articles/what-is-the-brrrr-method/.

Birk, C. 2025. "Complete Guide to the VA Home Loan." Veterans United Home Loans, August 1. https://www.veteransunited.com/va-loans/.

Bitton, D. 2023. "How to Find Tenants: Everything You Need to Know." DoorLoop Hubs, April 3. https://www.doorloop.com/hub/find-tenants.

Blankenship, M. 2023a. "7 BRRRR Method Risks You Should Know Before Investing." Call Porter, October 6. https://callporter.com/blog/brrrr-method-risks/.

Blankenship, M. 2023b. "The BRRRR Method vs. Flix & Flip: What's The Difference?" Call Porter, October 19. https://callporter.com/blog/the-brrrr-method-vs-flix-flip/.

Blankenship, M. 2024a. "5 Common Types of Real Estate Investing Contracts." Call Porter, March 1. https://callporter.com/blog/real-estate-investing-contracts/.

Blankenship, M. 2024b. "7 Real Estate Investing Calculators You Can Use for Free." Call Porter, December 31. https://callporter.com/blog/real-estate-investing-calculators/.

Boldyreff, K. 2020. "House Hacking 101: What It Is and How It Works." Northpointe.com, May 28. https://www.northpointe.com/learn/homes-real-estate/house-hacking-101-what-it-is-and-how-it-works/.

Brock, M. 2024. "What Is a Real Estate Portfolio and How Do You Build a Collection of Real Estate Investments?" Rocket Mortgage, March 27. https://www.rocketmortgage.com/learn/real-estate-portfolio.

Cartier, B. 2024. "Rental Property Accounting & Bookkeeping 101: Landlord's Guide." *Stessa*, December 23. https://www.stessa.com/blog/rental-property-accounting-101/.

Casago. 2024. "What Makes a Good Airbnb Property? A Guide to Amenities, Fees & More." Casago, September 1. https://casago.com/blog/airbnb-property-guide/.

Cepf, L. G. T., and M. Grace. 2025. "Finding the Right Real Estate Agent: Everything You Need to Know." Business Insider, April 11. https://www.businessinsider.com/personal-finance/mortgages/how-to-find-real-estate-agent.

Chen, J. 2024. "Multiple Listing Service (MLS): Definition, Benefits, and Fees." *Investopedia*, July 9. https://www.investopedia.com/terms/m/multiple-listing-service-mls.asp.

Collins, D. 2023. "What Is Wholesale Real Estate? This Guide Will Help You Understand the Basics, How the Selling Process Works, and Best Practices." December 21. https://www.rocketmortgage.com/learn/wholesale-real-estate.

Conde, A. 2023. "What Is a Real Estate Partnership?" SmartAsset, October 20. https://smartasset.com/investing/real-estate-partnership.

Crace, M. 2024. "Hard Money Loans, Unlike Traditional Loans, Are Based on the Collateral That Secures the Loan." Rocket Mortgage, February 22. https://www.rocketmortgage.com/learn/hard-money-loans/.

Dar, S. 2025. "Why Landlords Need a Separate Bank Account for Rental Property." Baselane, May 28. https://www.baselane.com/resources/separate-bank-account-for-rental-property/.

Davis, M. 2025a. "How to Find Your Return on Investment (ROI) in Real Estate." *Investopedia*, June 1. https://www.investopedia.com/articles/basics/11/calculate-roi-real-estate-investments.asp.

Davis, M. 2025b. "Real Estate Agent vs. Mortgage Broker: What's the Difference?" *Investopedia*, March 14. https://www.investopedia.com/articles/financialca reers/10/real-estate-agent-mortgage-broker.asp.

Dehan, A. 2025. "Hard Money Lending: Guide to Hard Money Loans." *Bankrate*, February 28. https://www.bankrate.com/mortgages/hard-money-lenders/.

Dixon, A. 2025. "Determining How Much You Should Charge for Rent." Smart Asset, January 30. Accessed July 12. https://smartasset.com/mortgage/how-much-you-should-charge-for-rent.

Dodge, A. 2025. "What Does Off-Market Mean in Real Estate?" FastExpert, April 25. https://www.fastexpert.com/blog/what-does-off-market-mean/.

DoorLoop. n.d. "The 2023 BRRRR Method Ultimate Guide for Real Estate Investors." Accessed July 8. https://www.doorloop.com/hubs/brrrr.

Dossey, J. 2023a. "4 Best Strategies to BRRRR Deals with No Money." Call Porter, October 12. https://callporter.com/blog/brrrr-method-with-no-money/.

Dossey, J. 2023b. "Investing in Real Estate: 7 Steps to Your First Deal." Call Porter, May 11. https://callporter.com/blog/guide-to-investing-in-real-estate/.

Drake Law. 2025. "Key Legal Factors to Consider Before Investing in Real Estate." June 16. https://www.drakelaw.ca/legal-insights/key-legal-factors-to-consider-before-investing-in-real-estate.

Duncan, A. 2024. "Staying Motivated in a Tough Market." Agent Monday, December 23. https://www.agentmonday.com/how-to-stay-motivated-in-a-tough-market/.

Evans, K. 2024. "Understanding Off-Market Listings: A Strategic Tool for Real Estate Agents." *Luxury Presence*, August 13. https://www.luxurypresence.com/blogs/off-market-listings/.

Fairless, J. 2022. "Real Estate Horror Stories from Five Active Investors." Best Ever Commercial Real Estate, June 9. https://www.bestevercre.com/blog/real-estate-horror-stories-five-active-investors.

Fraraccio, M. 2025. "Buying an Existing Business? How to Finance Your Purchase." CO—by US Chamber of Commerce, January 31. https://www.uschamber.com/co/run/business-financing/financing-buying-an-existing-business.

Freitas, T. 2025. "What Is an FHA Loan?" *Bankrate*, May 9. https://www.bankrate.com/mortgages/what-is-an-fha-loan/.

Gibson, J. 2025. "Factors to Consider Before You Refinance Your Mortgage." *Investopedia*, March 24. https://www.investopedia.com/mortgage/refinance/9-things-to-know-before-you-refinance-mortgage/.

The Ginther Group. 2024. "Setting Real Estate Goals: Buying, Selling, or Investing." December 23. https://theginthergroup.com/tips/buying-selling-investing-goals/.

Goade, C. 2023. "Is a Stack of Cash Better than Slow but Steady Returns? A Look at Flipping and the BRRRR Method." BiggerPockets, November 5. https://www.biggerpockets.com/blog/flip-vs-brrrr-real-estate.

Goff, K. 2023. "What Is the 70% Rule in House Flipping?" *Bankrate*, February 21. https://www.bankrate.com/real-estate/70-percent-rule-house-flipping/.

Grace, M., and A. J. Yale. 2025. "Understanding the Loan-to-Value Ratio (LTV) and What It Means for Mortgage Borrowers." Business Insider, March 28. https://www.businessinsider.com/personal-finance/mortgages/loan-to-value-ratio-mortgage-refinancing.

Graham, K. 2024. "An FHA Loan Is a Government-Backed Loan That Allows You to Buy a Home with Less Strict Financial Requirements." Rocket Mortgage, November 20. https://www.rocketmortgage.com/learn/fha-loans.

Gratton, P. 2025a. "Flipping Houses: How It Works, Where to Start, and 5 Mistakes to Avoid." *Investopedia*, February 6. https://www.investopedia.com/articles/mortgages-real-estate/08/house-flip.asp.

Gratton, P. 2025b. "What Is Depreciation Recapture?" *Investopedia*, February 25. https://www.investopedia.com/terms/d/depreciationrecapture.asp

Harris, V. 2019. "How to Get Started in Real Estate Investing: Your 90 Day Plan." Mashvisor Real Estate, January 17. https://www.mashvisor.com/blog/get-started-real-estate-investing-90-day-plan/.

Hayes, A. 2024. "Loan-to-Value (LTV) Ratio: What It Is, How to Calculate, Example." *Investopedia*, September 26. https://www.investopedia.com/terms/l/loantovalue.asp.

Heath, K. 2024. "Lender or Realtor: Who Should You Talk to First Before Buying a House? FastExpert, March 13. https://www.fastexpert.com/blog/lender-or-realtor-who-to-talk-first-before-buying-house/.

Hendricks, M. 2023. "How Private Money Lending Works." SmartAsset, March 19. https://smartasset.com/personal-loans/how-private-money-lending-works.

Henson, T. 2024. "Flipping vs. Renting—Which Real Estate Strategy Is Best for Long-term Gains." Beach Front Property Management Inc., December 18. https://bfpminc.com/flipping-vs-renting-which-real-estate-strategy-is-best-for-long-term-gains/.

Hrovat, J. 2024. "Maximizing Short-Term Rental with the BRRRR Method." UpRev, October 15. https://www.uprev.co/post/maximizing-short-term-rental-brrrr-method.

Huff, J. 2023. "BRRRR vs. Flipping: A Comparison of Real Estate Investment Strategies." Jacobs & Co. Real Estate, November 8. https://www.jacobsandco.com/blog/brrrr-vs-flipping-a-comparison-of-real-estate-investment-strategies/.

Hughes, E. 2025. "Completing My First BRRRR Property." Rental Income Advisors, April 28. https://www.rentalincomeadvisors.com/blog/my-first-brrrr-prop erty.

Internal Revenue Service. n.d. "Tips on Rental Real Estate Income, Deductions and Recordkeeping." Accessed July 14. https://www.irs.gov/businesses/small-busi nesses-self-employed/tips-on-rental-real-estate-income-deductions-and-recordkeeping.

Internal Revenue Service. 2024. "Publication 527: Residential Rental Property." https://www.irs.gov/publications/p527.

The Investopedia Team. 2023. "4 Tips for Joining an Investment Club." *Investopedia*, September 16. https://www.investopedia.com/articles/01/062001.asp.

Jamal, A. 2021. "How to Diversify Your Real Estate Portfolio." *Forbes*, August 3. https://www.forbes.com/sites/forbesbooksauthors/2021/08/03/how-to-diver sify-your-real-estate-portfolio/.

Johnson, M. 2023. "6 Renovation Projects That Pay Off for ROI, According to an Expert." *Architectural Digest*, September 25. https://www.architecturaldigest. com/story/renovation-projects-and-their-roi-according-to-an-expert.

Jones, R. n.d. "Setting Effective Property Investment Goals: How to Achieve Success in 2025." Property Investments UK. https://www.propertyinvest mentsuk.co.uk/5-steps-property-success-goal-setting/.

J. P. Morgan Chase. 2023. "How to Use the BRRRR Method in Real Estate." March 31. https://www.chase.com/personal/mortgage/education/buying-a-home/ brrrr-method.

Kagan, J. 2021. "VA Loan: Definition, Eligibility Requirements, Types & Terms." *Investopedia*, November 27. https://www.investopedia.com/terms/v/valoan.asp.

Karani, A. 2020. "How to Evaluate a Neighborhood Before Investing." Mashvisor Real Estate, December 27. https://www.mashvisor.com/blog/evaluate-a-neigh borhood-investing/.

Knaack, E. 2024. "Building a Successful REI Team & Keeping Them Accountable." *Deal Machine* (blog), May 16. https://www.dealmachine.com/blog/how-to-build-a-team.

Kopp, C. M. 2020. "1% Rule in Real Estate: What It Is, How It Works, Examples." *Investopedia*, November 11. https://www.investopedia.com/terms/o/one-percent-rule.asp.

Langager, C. 2025. "Reducing or Avoiding Capital Gains Tax on Home Sales." *Investopedia*, February 23. https://www.investopedia.com/ask/answers/06/capi talgainhomesale.asp.

Lecko, D. 2021. "What Is ARV in Real Estate & How to Calculate." *Deal Machine* (blog), December 23. https://www.dealmachine.com/blog/what-is-arv-in-real-estate.

Lombardo, T. 2024. "Maximizing Returns: The Power of Evaluating Neighborhoods for Residential Real Estate Investment Success." Carolina Venture REI, February 5. https://carolinaventurerei.com/evaluating-neighbor hoods-for-residential-real-estate-investment-success/.

Lubin, D. 2023. "3 Types of Loans to Maximize the BRRRR Method." Kiavi Funding, Inc., December 15. https://www.kiavi.com/blog/three-types-of-loans-to-maximize-the-brrrr-method.

Lubin, D. 2024. "How to Calculate a Profitable BRRRR Property." Kiavi Funding, Inc., March 25. https://www.kiavi.com/blog/how-to-calculate-a-profitable-brrrr-property.

The Luxury Playbook. 2025. "10 Best Real Estate Investment Exit Strategies (+ Examples)." April 17. https://theluxuryplaybook.com/real-estate-investment-exit-strategies/.

Maldonado, J. D. 2022. "What's the Story of Your First Deal?" BiggerPockets, June 22. https://www.biggerpockets.com/forums/48/topics/1046282-whats-the-story-of-your-first-deal.

Martin, E. J. 2025. "What Is a Private Mortgage Lender?" *Bankrate*, March 10. https://www.bankrate.com/mortgages/what-is-a-private-mortgage-lender/.

Moeen, A. 2024. "ARV Calculator—After Repair Value." Omni Calculator, April 23. https://www.omnicalculator.com/finance/arv

Moore, A. 2024. "Case Study: A Real Estate Success Story with Hard Money Funding." Lending Bee, May 13. https://lendingbeeinc.com/blog/case-study-a-real-estate-success-story-with-hard-money-funding.

myRealPage. 2025. "Why Reinvesting in Your Real Estate Business Is Essential and How to Do It." myRealPage, May 5. https://myrealpage.com/real-estate-market ing/reinvesting-real-estate-business-essential/.

National Association of Realtors. 2024. "Highlights from the Profile of Home Buyers and Sellers." November 4. https://www.nar.realtor/research-and-statistics/research-reports/highlights-from-the-profile-of-home-buyers-and-sellers.

National Association of Realtors. 2025. "Remodeling Impact." April 9. https://www.nar.realtor/research-and-statistics/research-reports/remodeling-impact.

Nesbit, J. 2025. "What Is the 70% Rule in House Flipping and Does It Show How Much to Pay for a Distressed Property?" Rocket Mortgage, February 19. https://www.rocketmortgage.com/learn/what-is-70-rule-in-house-flipping.

Nichols, B. 2023. "Mastering BRRRR: The Power of Refinancing in Real Estate." *Deal Machine* (blog), December 3. https://www.dealmachine.com/blog/master ing-brrrr-refinancing-in-real-estate-investing.

Nicola, G. 2025. "Flipping vs. BRRR: Which Real Estate Investment Strategy Is Right for You?" Tallbox, March 28. https://www.tallboxdesign.com/flipping-vs-brrrr-which-strategy-is-for-you/.

Nock Deighton. n.d. "ROI (Return on Investment) Calculator." Accessed June 29. https://www.nockdeighton.co.uk/investment-calculator.

Nowacki, L. 2024a. "Breaking Down the 1% Rule in Real Estate: What You Should Know Before Investing." Rocket Mortgage, February 27. https://www.rocket mortgage.com/learn/1-rule-real-estate.

Nowacki, L. 2024b. "Understand the BRRRR Method of Real Estate Investments." Rocket Mortgage, May 16. https://www.rocketmortgage.com/learn/brrrr.

Olson, L. n.d. "10 Types of Insurance for Real Estate Investors to Consider." Obie Insurance. Accessed July 2. https://www.obieinsurance.com/blog/insurance-for-real-estate-investors.

Pallardy, C. 2025. "How to Find and Buy Off-Market Homes." Investopedia, March 17. https://www.investopedia.com/articles/personal-finance/121415/how-find-and-buy-offmarket-homes.asp.

Paquette, A. 2019. "Success Story of the Week: Will FHA work for you?" Athena Paquette (blog), August 8. https://athenapaquette.com/success-story-of-the-week-will-fha-work-for-you/.

Parker, T. 2025. "Home Improvements That Require Permits." Investopedia, April 17. https://www.investopedia.com/financial-edge/1012/home-improvements-that-require-permits.aspx.

Peterson, L. 2025. "How many hours per week does it take to manage a successful Airbnb?" L'abode Accommodation, April 21. https://labodeaccommodation.com.au/time-spent-on-an-airbnb/.

Pisano, N. 2024. "Residential Real Estate Investing in 2024: More Rent Money, More Rental Problems." Clever, July 22. https://listwithclever.com/research/residential-real-estate-investing-2024/.

Plati, A. 2024. "How to Conduct a Real Estate Market Study: The Perfect Guide." October 21. https://www.netquest.com/en/blog/how-to-conduct-real-estate-market-study-perfect-guide.

Ramsey Solutions. 2025. "How to Create a Home Renovation Budget." March 27. https://www.ramseysolutions.com/real-estate/home-renovation-budget?srsltid=AfmBOorAz3wQZNv1mvhEhlIaFeKSAP-z-S5H9BlBA5AMzkdS0Ifp YAbS.

Reiff, N. 2025. "Do-It-Yourself Projects to Boost Home Value." Investopedia, March 18. https://www.investopedia.com/articles/mortgages-real-estate/08/diy-home-projects.asp.

Rodriguez, C. 2024. "To Flip or to BRRRR?" BiggerPockets, March 9. https://www.biggerpockets.com/forums/48/topics/1127968-to-flip-or-to-brrrr.

Rogers, E. 2025. "What You Need to Know About Building Wealth with the BRRRR Method in St. George." Red Rock Real Estate, February 3. https://www.relocate tosunnystgeorge.com/blog/what-you-need-to-know-about-building-wealth-with-the-brrrr-method-in-st-george.

Rosenberg, E. 2025. "Ultimate Guide to BRRRR Method For Real Estate Investment." Baselane, May 14. https://www.baselane.com/resources/brrrr-method-for-real-estate/.

Segal, T. 2024. "Hard Money Loan: Definition, Uses, and Pros & Cons." *Investopedia*, May 7. https://www.investopedia.com/terms/h/hard_money_loan.asp.

Segal, T. 2025. "Federal Housing Administration (FHA) Loan: Requirements, Limits, How to Qualify." *Investopedia*, March 27. https://www.investopedia. com/terms/f/fhaloan.asp.

Shehaj, E. 2022. "The Ultimate 60-Day Action Plan for the Paralyzed Newbie Longing for a First Deal." BiggerPockets, July 29. https://www.biggerpockets. com/blog/60-day-newbie-action-plan.

Shour, E. 2025. "Should You Hire a Property Manager? The Pros & Cons." Stessa, April 15. https://www.stessa.com/blog/should-you-hire-property-manager/.

Shugrue, D. 2023. "How to Plan Your Home Renovation Costs." *Budget Dumpster* (blog), December 4. https://www.budgetdumpster.com/blog/budget-home-renovation.

Sprenkle, B. 2024. "The Dilemma on Whether to Refinance or Sell." American Apartment Owners Association, June 4. https://american-apartment-owners-association.org/property-management/the-dilemma-on-whether-to-refinance-or-sell/?srsltid=AfmBOorvn4BfX0OGOJGafoPelEyfNera-1-FN3rAl WXGI5QpqvG5EAxY.

Stammers, R. 2021. "Should You Buy and Hold Real Estate or Flip Properties?" *Investopedia*, January 27. https://www.investopedia.com/articles/mortgages-real-estate/08/flipping-flip-properties.asp.

Stohler, N. 2024. "How to Find Off-Market Properties: 13 Winning Methods." Azibo, June 28. https://www.azibo.com/blog/how-to-find-off-market-proper ties.

Subel, M. 2024. "Home Remodeling Steps: A Checklist to Help Plan and Organize Your Renovation." Dave Fox, August 29. https://www.davefox.com/resource-center/whole-home-remodeling-steps-checklist.

Talbot, A. 2025. "What Is 'House Hacking' and How Is It Helping Millennials and Gen Z Buy Houses?" Webster First Federal Credit Union, January 22. https:// www.websterfirst.com/blog/what-is-house-hacking-definition/.

Travelers. 2023. "10 Common Rental Property Repairs Landlords Need to Know About." February 28. https://www.travelers.com/resources/home/landlords/10-common-rental-property-repairs-landlords-need-to-know-about.

Turner, B. 2020. "The BRRRR Origin Story: How I Discovered This Amazing—No Money—Real Estate Strategy." BiggerPockets, July 11. https://www.bigger pockets.com/blog/brrrr-origin-story.

Vazquez, J. 2024. "The Difference Between Rehabbing a Flip, Short-Term Rental, Corporate Rental, Long-Term Rental, and BRRRR Strategy." Graystone Investment Group, August 30. https://graystoneig.com/articles/the-difference-between-rehabbing-a-flip-short-term-rental-corporate-rental-long-term-rental-and-brrrr-strategy.

Villegas, F. 2024. "Real Estate Market Analysis: What It Is & How to Do It." QuestionPro, April 10. https://www.questionpro.com/blog/real-estate-market-analysis/.

Wall Street Prep. 2024. "After-Repair Value (ARV)." February 20. https://www.wall streetprep.com/knowledge/after-repair-value-arv/.

Webber, M. R. 2024. "The Top Renovations That Increase Home Value in 2024." *Bankrate*, May 13. https://www.bankrate.com/homeownership/home-renova tions-that-return-the-most-at-resale/.

Welty, S. 2025. "Short-Term Rental vs. Long-Term Rental: 12 Things to Know." Good Life Property Management, May 19. https://www.goodlifemgmt.com/ blog/short-term-rental-vs-long-term-rental/.

White, J. 2025. "What's a Good Return on Investment (ROI)?" SmartAsset, May 28. https://smartasset.com/investing/whats-a-good-return-on-investment-roi.

White, M., and A. Conde. 2024. "How to Start Wholesaling Real Estate in 7 Steps." Smart Asset, July 29. https://smartasset.com/mortgage/how-to-get-started-wholesaling-real-estate.

Williams, T. 2022. "Look for these 12 red flags to avoid hiring bad contractors." Architectural Digest, March 14. https://www.architecturaldigest.com/story/ bad-contractors-red-flags-warning-signs.

Wood, R. W. 2024. "What Is a 1031 Exchange? Know the Rules." *Investopedia*, December 16. https://www.investopedia.com/financial-edge/0110/10-things-to-know-about-1031-exchanges.aspx.

Woodman, C. 2023. "How to Scale Your Real Estate Portfolio." New Silver, May 24. https://newsilver.com/the-lender/how-to-scale-your-real-estate-portfolio/.

Woodman, C. 2025. "Over Leveraged Real Estate—What Is It and How to Avoid It." New Silver, March 24. https://newsilver.com/the-lender/over-leveraged-real-estate/.

Woodward, E. 2024. "The BRRRR Method: What It Means and What It Stands For." *Bankrate*, February 23. https://www.bankrate.com/real-estate/brrrr-method-in-real-estate/.

Young Entrepreneur Council. 2023. "How Real Estate Investors Can Find Off-Market Properties." *Forbes*, February 14. https://www.forbes.com/councils/theyec/2023/02/14/how-real-estate-investors-can-find-off-market-properties/.

Zinn, D. 2024. "How to Flip a House: A Beginner's Guide." *Bankrate*, July 8. https://www.bankrate.com/real-estate/flipping-houses/.

IMAGE REFERENCES

Anke, Peggy. 2018. *Airbnb*. Image. Pixabay. May 19. https://pixabay.com/photos/airbnb-air-bnb-apartment-3399753/.

Cytonn Photography. 2018. *Two People Shaking Hands*. Image. Unsplash. March 23. https://unsplash.com/photos/two-people-shaking-hands-n95VMLxqM2I.

Danilyuk, Pavel. 2021. *Couple Holding Blueprint of a House*. Image. Pexels. May 18. https://www.pexels.com/photo/couple-holding-blueprint-of-a-house-7937668/

Kindel Media. 2021. *People Holding a Key*. Image. Pexels. April 16. https://www.pexels.com/photo/people-holding-a-key-7579192/.

Lehner, Stefan. 2021. *A Room That Has Some Tools in It*. Image. Unsplash. October 18. https://unsplash.com/photos/a-room-that-has-some-tools-in-it-biRt6RXejuk.

McBee, David. 2018. *High Angle Shot of Suburban Neighborhood*. Image. Pexels. October 28. https://www.pexels.com/photo/high-angle-shot-of-suburban-neighborhood-1546168/.

Mils, Alexander. 2019. *Fan of 100 U. S. Dollar Banknotes*. Image. Unsplash. March 27. https://unsplash.com/photos/fan-of-100-us-dollar-banknotes-lCPhGxs7pww.

RDNE Stock Project. 2021. *Person Wearing Silver Ring Holding Red Pen on White Printer Paper*. Image. Pexels. May 25. https://www.pexels.com/photo/person-wearing-silver-ring-holding-red-pen-on-white-printer-paper-8052843/

Thirdman. 2021. *Shallow Focus Photo of a Realtor Posting a Sold Sticker*. Image. Pexels. June 24. https://www.pexels.com/photo/shallow-focus-photo-of-a-realtor-posting-a-sold-sticker-8470803/.

ALSO BY FRANK EBERSTADT

How to launch your own Airbnb empire from scratch — no property management experience required.

Data from Stratos Jet Charters show that **approximately 14,000 new hosts are joining Airbnb...** *every month.*

So if you plan on turning a decent profit with your Airbnb listing, you will have to find creative ways to stand out from the competition.

The good news is there's nothing to worry about.

Because the truth is anyone can start their own Airbnb rental business.

All you need are **practical strategies and principles that have been proven to work repeatedly.**

In this book, you'll discover:

- The simple **6-step framework for launching an Airbnb listing from scratch**
- The 4 primary types of Airbnb accommodations and which one you should use for your property

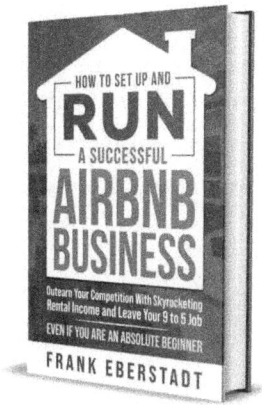

- How to calculate the profitability of your Airbnb listing — always look at these 5 factors
- **Airbnb Insurance: what's included and what additional coverage you might need**
- The 7 best safety tips for Airbnb hosts
- **The subtle difference between a house manual and house rules**
- **3 core components of any effective Airbnb listing** — focus on THIS element above all others
- How to automate these behind-the-scenes processes for your Airbnb business
- **9 signs that starting your own short-term rental business is the perfect fit for you**

And much more!

There's no secret "hack" to winning on Airbnb.

And unlike other guides that promote overly complex strategies filled with technical terminology... this book is designed specifically for *anyone* to understand.

So whether you're already an Airbnb host or have just discovered how Airbnb works, you'll have all the fundamental knowledge you need to start earning rental income on the side.

Scan the QR code below and get your copy now.

Unlock the secrets to skyrocketing your rental income and bookings with this comprehensive guide to mastering Airbnb!

Your Airbnb property isn't just bricks and mortar—it's a treasure chest of untapped potential. If you only had the right map to guide you, imagine the possibilities.

You could unlock your property's full potential, transform your Airbnb business into a consistent income generator, and finally leave behind the days of just scraping by.

This is where Frank Eberstadt steps in.

He's back with his latest book that promises to be the companion that steers you beyond Airbnb basics and puts you confidently in the driver's seat.

Inside, you will discover:

- **How to research your market effectively and outsmart your competition** – identify your unique selling proposition and elevate your Airbnb above the competition!
- **An arsenal of advanced pricing strategies tailored for different seasons and property types** – navigate the tumultuous tides of seasonal demands and make sure your rental rates are always on point
- **The magic of transitioning and diversification to ensure consistent income** – you no longer need to worry about slow seasons

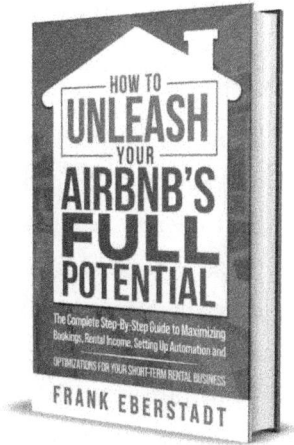

- **The power of data analytics and metrics to make informed business decisions** – drive informed decisions to boost your income
- **Tips and tricks to optimize your Airbnb listing and attract more bookings** – make your listing so appealing that guests can't resist clicking "book now"!
- **Secrets to building a stellar reputation and becoming a beloved Superhost** – charm your guests and earn glowing 5-star reviews with ease!
- **Techniques to automate your Airbnb business and save valuable time** – imagine spending less time on admin and more time enjoying the fruits of your success

And much more!

Wave goodbye to frustration and uncertainty – step into a future where your Airbnb investment transforms into a consistent income-generating machine!

It is time to up your Airbnb game.

Scan the QR code below and get your copy now.

ABOUT THE AUTHOR

Frank Eberstadt is an accommodation manager and bestselling author of books on Airbnb and real estate investing.

His books address property management and business growth in short-term rentals, guiding readers to seek and capitalize on opportunities in the market while nurturing successful businesses along the way.

Frank is the accommodation manager for an investment group operating hotels and motels in Australia. He has established his own successful Airbnb business, and has grown his portfolio to six properties. Frank began his first Airbnb business from the ground up and knows how hard it can be to break into property listings and attract guests. Using his extensive experience in the accommodation industry, his aim is to lay out a clear, step-by-step path that even complete newbies can follow to success.

Frank's interest in vacation property stems from his many years traveling as a solo backpacker, something he now does with his family. These two very different traveling experiences have fed into his awareness of what makes a successful vacation rental, and have been key to his success as an Airbnb business owner.

Frank still loves to travel, and enjoys surfing, but more than anything, he loves to spend quality time with his family, no matter where their adventures take them.

www.ingramcontent.com/pod-product-compliance
Lightning Source LLC
Chambersburg PA
CBHW030453210326
41597CB00013B/645